Making Cities Work

Acknowledgements

This book was produced with the financial assistance of Clear Channel Worldwide and the help of Clear Channel staff. In particular, the authors wish to pay special thanks to James Craven who did a huge amount of work to prepare and contribute to the case studies and source so many of the photographs. We also want to thank Daniel Cukierman who is one of the world's leading experts on railways and transport systems and who contributed to the 'Arriving in the City' section of this book. Thanks should also go to Jennie Calver and Jenny Hazel for their work as picture researchers. Finally, a big thank you to all those at John Wiley and Sons who were involved in bringing the book to publication - in particular Mariangela Palazzi-Williams, who really made this book a reality, and Abigail Grater - and to the designer Mario Bettella of Artmedia Press, for their hard work and dedication.

Published in Great Britain in 2004 by Wiley-Academy, a division of John Wiley & Sons Ltd

Other Wiley Editorial Offices

John Wiley & Sons Inc., 111 River Street, Hoboken, NJ 07030, USA

Jossey-Bass, 989 Market Street, San Francisco, CA 94103-1741, USA

Wiley-VCH Verlag GmbH, Boschstr. 12, D-69469 Weinheim, Germany

John Wiley & Sons Australia Ltd, 33 Park Road, Milton, Queensland 4064, Australia

John Wiley & Sons (Asia) Pte Ltd, 2 Clementi Loop #02-01, Jin Xing Distripark, Singapore 129809

John Wiley & Sons Canada Ltd, 22 Worcester Road, Etobicoke, Ontario, Canada M9W 1L1

ISBN 0470-84681-X

Design and Prepress: ARTMEDIA PRESS Ltd, London

Printed and bound in Italy by Conti Tipocolor

Making Cities Work

George Hazel
Roger Parry

WILEY-ACADEMY

Contents

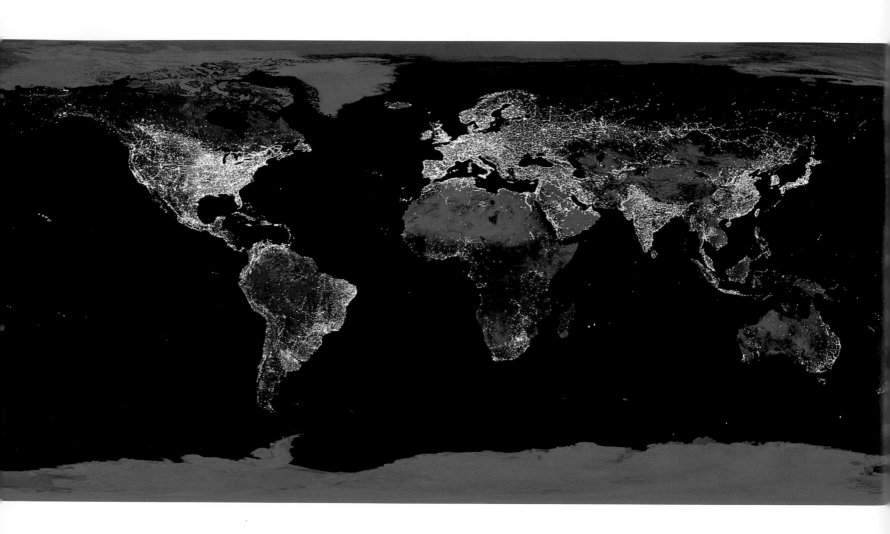

Any extraterrestrial observer would note and marvel at the way our cities dominate the globe

Introduction

More than 2,000 million people now live in cities: a third of the world's population. In the 1950s, only some 200 million were city dwellers. In just half a century cities have expanded by a factor of 10. In 50 years time, more than 60% of humanity – some 5,000 million people – will live in a city.

Cities now define the human race and indeed define the planet Earth. Any extra-terrestrial observer would note and marvel at the way our cities dominate the globe, long before they discovered much more about us.

What we now think of as a city really started with the Greeks about 5,000 years ago, as people left the land and looked for ways of organising their society. In the 100,000-year history of human beings, cities are a relatively recent development.

Already, 2,000 years ago Rome was home to 100,000 people. When William the Conqueror rode into London around 1,000 years ago, it was then the world's largest city boasting a population of 150,000. By 1950 New York had that honour with 12 million inhabitants. Today Tokyo is the biggest and home to nearly 30 million.

There are now 20 cities with a population of 12 million plus and more than 50 cities with a population of more than 5 million. Human effort on this scale is easily visible from the Moon.

Cities are the human race at its very best and very worst. Inspiring social, technological and artistic innovations and creating depressing collections of poverty, disease and crime. Cities cannot be ignored. Their growth trend cannot be reversed. We must find ways to make cities better places.

Tokyo is the biggest city in the world and home to nearly 30 million people

The Car

If there is one thing that defines the city today and which will be the single greatest influence on urban life over the next 100 years, it is the car.

In 1900 the world had 100,000 cars. By 1950 it was 50 million. By the year 2000 it was 500 million. By 2050 it is likely to be in excess of a 1,000 million. Most of those cars at some time enter cities. Cities have to accommodate the automobile.

Pollution, social alienation, slums, urban blight, the decay of city centres, the sprawl of the suburbs, not to mention gridlock and road rage, all these problems can be laid at the wheels of the automobile. Yet the car is also the most socially liberating machine ever invented and car ownership the main aspiration for the majority of the world's population.

In 1909, Henry Ford, the founder of the Ford Motor Company had a vision for the future of automobile production:

I will build a motorcar for the great multitude…When I am through, everybody will be able to afford one, and everyone will have one. Horses will disappear from our highways, the automobile will be taken for granted…

In 1932, Aldous Huxley's novel of the future, *Brave New World*, the creator of the automobile actually becomes a deity. The story was set in the year AF 632, ("After Ford"), which was 632 years after the birth of the first Ford Model T car in 1908. Ford is the God of Huxley's predicted society.

By 2050 there are likely to be in excess of 1,000 million cars

Finding a balance between pedestrians and cars in the city presents a challenge

Achieving a Balance

How do we design and operate cities to balance the conflicting demands upon them?

We have a strong desire to live in large urban communities. Once there we want to find work, to be entertained, to have the convenience of shops and services and just have the company of others. We all seem to believe that being in a city will increase our overall quality of life, although evidence in many cases seems to support the opposite.

Making Cities Work

This book showcases ideas from around the world that have enabled cities to work more successfully and have enhanced the quality of life for city dwellers. They are demonstrations of excellence and best practice; ideas in action, not just theory. This book does not pretend to deliver a comprehensive city solution, but simply to present a collection of working initiatives.

Many of the ideas are linked to more effective transport systems, as moving people around is a key challenge. Others are examples of redesigning the urban environment to make it more sympathetic to the needs of people and more human in dimension.

Putting these ideas into action is often the work of a single individual, rather than a civic group. It requires personal ownership, combined with vision, grit and determination to get things done.

Coming to terms with the city is what this book is about. It is organised into three sections: Arriving in the City, Enjoying the City and Getting Around the City.

1. Arriving in the City

Arriving in the City profiles some of the world's most successful gateways and transport interchanges. First impressions really count and a city that demonstrates a commitment to quality and accessibility already starts with a huge advantage. Cities are, by their very nature, not just places where people live, but they are destinations that many more people visit for a brief period. They have to arrive and leave. To do this in style and comfort creates a positive first and lasting impression of the city as well as the arrival point.

- TGV stations in southern France make passengers feel good about using railways as well as creating a positive image for the local cities and surrounding areas
- Chep Lap Kok Airport in Hong Kong makes departing passengers feel closer to their planes and arriving passengers closer to the city within a high-quality, enjoyable space
- The dramatic reconstruction of Grand Central Station in New York brings new life, not just to the railways, but to a large section in the heart of the city
- The Yokohama Ferry Terminal brings the sea to the city and the city to the sea in a welcoming and exciting environment for both traveller and locals alike.

A variety of landmarks welcome visitors to cities all around the world – from a gigantic statue to a busy station

Two ways of enjoying city life; relaxing in a café and shopping

2. Enjoying the City

Enjoying the City highlights the ingenious approaches that are taken to parks, shopping malls and public spaces. It is a large number of small-scale amenities that make a city fun to be in.

- The Steel Arbour is the centrepiece of the new Brisbane South Bank and is a fine example of the reclamation and rediscovery of a former urban wasteland
- The reclaiming of Copenhagen city squares, putting people first – before cars
- The redevelopment of Faneuil Hall in Boston has transformed historic buildings and brought them back to life and relevance in the 21st century
- The dramatic creation of the outdoors inside a Toronto mall shows us that we do not need to be limited in our imagination due to severe weather changes
- The Rocks in Sydney have transformed derelict warehouses into an area of entertainment and reclaimed a commercial zone for the population.

3. Getting Around the City

The third section, *Getting Around the City*, addresses the biggest challenge for most urban leaders – how to move people around in safety, comfort and speed. This is the area where political trade-offs are at their most acute – the pedestrian versus the car, pollution versus clean air, communities versus roads. It is not just a matter of huge public investment. It is also a matter of ideas and good operating practices.

- The low cost Edinburgh 'Greenways' system to get buses moving through the reallocation of road space
- The Legible City in Bristol has taken the theoretical basis of the city's diverse parts and linked them with consistent information and identity

- The Rennes bicycle scheme and the transformation of Groningen, where 60% of all journeys are now made by bicycle, illustrate how the bicycle can play a major role
- The stylish Strasbourg trams have revolutionised travel patterns by attracting car users in a very short time
- Road pricing in Singapore has been a successful strategy for many years, reducing city centre congestion.

A book like this will always raise the criticism: 'You have left out much better examples.' This is almost certainly true. Developments like the River Walk in San Antonio, the cycle paths in Toronto and the docks in Cape Town are all examples of clever, successful projects that enhance city life. But our objectives are to stimulate discussion, not provide all the answers.

Public transport can add colour to urban life

Generating New Ideas

This book is intended to make people think and to encourage the exchange of ideas. Our examples are posted on a web site www.makingcitieswork.com. We would like people to look at this and to prepare and post their own examples of excellence. Readers will be able to enter an international competition for the best example via the website.

George Hazel and Roger Parry
October 2003

VENICE

THE CLASSIC CASE STUDY

A distinguished American reporter arrived in Venice to cover international events in the city and telexed the now famous epithet home to New York – 'Arrived Venice, streets full of water, please advise!'

This situation endures to the present day as Venice's principal defining characteristic. Why then include it as a paradigm for enjoying the modern city when almost every other city has few if any canals? The answer lies in the degree to which Venice has managed and enhanced its unique sense of place and community to provide the conditions for modern metropolitan life.

Above *The evolution in life to adapt to canals creates opportunities for social interaction*
Opposite *The train approaches Venice on a causeway that crosses the lagoon*

First, and perhaps most startling, are the lessons that road based cities can learn from Venice in creating the conditions for modern urbanity. Although there are other cities with canals, not even Amsterdam is so completely surrounded and interpenetrated by water.

Throughout its history, Venice has developed sophisticated and ingenious systems of water transport to meet the needs of its citizens. Modern Venice has fire boats, police launches, removal boats, delivery boats and of course *gondolas*, *vaporetti* (water buses) and *motoscafi* – surely the most elegant and luxurious taxis in the world. Where boats cannot go, goods are unloaded onto the canal side to be portered the final few metres to their destination by handcart. In the simple acceptance that the final few metres of delivery must be made by barrow, Venice has avoided the greatest cancer afflicting modern cities – the congestion brought about by the demand for universal accessibility. Think how much better our cities would be if service vehicles had to unload their deliveries at the end of our greatest streets, ferrying goods the final few metres by hand cart. There is no reason why this could not happen in all major cities. It is only misplaced ideals of efficiency that demand that vehicles can drive right up to reach their final destination. The evolution in life to adapt to canals not carriage ways also creates opportunities for social interaction whether with the porters with their barrows or waiting for the two-man gondola ferries to cross the Grand Canal to avoid a long walk to the nearest bridge. There is no doubt that these aspects of Venetian life greatly enhance urban vitality through the interaction of people as they go about their daily lives. Of course these conditions for public life can flourish because all Venetians have no choice but to leave their cars outside the city and use the water-based public transport and their feet to get around!

Venice has some very fine big tourist civic set pieces, but the richness of Venice lies behind the public façade.

As the Venetian state developed the civic *palazzi* and *arsenale* as symbols of state power, the general population settled on the smaller islands of the lagoon and on those fields – *campi* – used for agricultural purposes. They constructed buildings on piles around the perimeter of each island, enclosing the central space, creating a sanctuary for family and animals. Gradually over time the building density around the perimeter intensified and the central area was paved over to create a public space at the heart of the community. These public spaces remain at the heart of Venetian life in the residential quarters of the city today often providing weekly or daily markets, newspaper stands, cafés for residents and crèches for children.

For the visitor interested in the urban life of Venice, they provide a charming diversion from the big-tourist sites of Piazza San Marco and the Canal Grande. Their origins are betrayed by their name, which usually begins with *campo* rather than the more usual *piazza* for square. Campo Santa Margherita is a typical example where visitors who quietly sip coffee and watch the world go by are treated with good-humoured tolerance and a welcoming *buongiorno*.

In counterpoint to these quiet residential *campi*, Venice has many fine squares. Some of the smaller squares exhibit quite particular characteristics to the outsider. To the interested observer of urban life, on first inspection, some Venetian squares are quiet and others very busy. On further inspection, some squares exhibit a distinct pattern of busy and quiet periods. Of course this relates to the normal cycle to be expected in any city: people having a coffee on the way to work, or at morning break, lunch or a drink with friends on the way home.

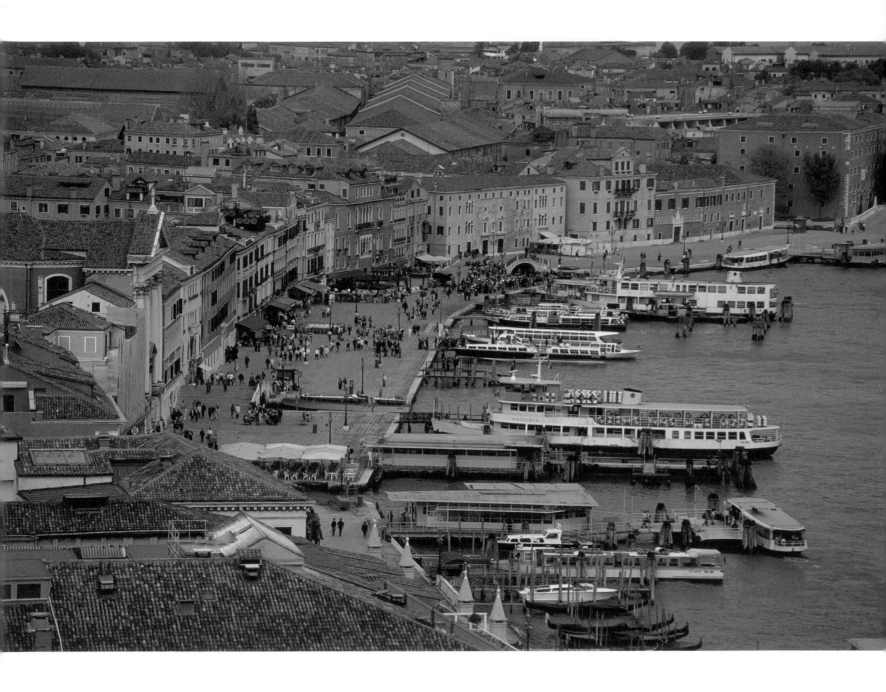

Modern Venice has fireboats, police launches, removal boats and of course water buses (vaporetti)

Left *Squares in Venice are a focal point for the whole community*
Right *Venetians have no choice but to leave their cars outside the city
and use water-based public transport*

The Grand Canal weaves through Venice

But some of the squares are very special, because they have a reputation among Venetians as destinations for informal conversations about business, projects and civic life away from the highly formal and structured mode of official life. People head for these 'talking squares' where they will have a coffee and walk around the square once or twice while formulating strategy for the forthcoming meetings or projects. These squares, like Piazza San Bartolomeo, are often close to civic buildings and exhibit extremes of tranquillity and vitality at different times.

For long periods of the day, they are extremely quiet – just a few residents and the independent tourist tired of the 'showpiece venues'. Gradually, however, by mid-morning, an air of expectation develops – cups are cleared away, tables cleaned, chairs tidied and, in no more than fifteen minutes, the square is crammed with smart official-looking people – loud greetings are exchanged, animated conversations break out everywhere at once and café owners move into overdrive as they attempt to meet demand – a deafening ensemble of concentrated animated humanity which lasts for maybe twenty minutes and then dies away as quickly as it began with just a few stragglers left perhaps hammering out the details of a business deal or agreeing diary dates. These are one or two of the many small delights of the Venice which awaits the interested observer prepared to spend more time in the city than a day trip from the Italian Lakes will permit.

How, then, to arrive? Perhaps best is by train, but some pre-planning is important for, if possible, it is best to arrive after a lengthy journey say from Milan on an old *expresso* (i.e. slow train) without air-conditioning and at the height of summer. After about three hours and many stops the ride becomes distinctly smoother and is accompanied by a noticeable increase in speed – the train has reached the causeway, which crosses the lagoon. To make up for the frustrations of irritating delays and obtuse scheduling, the driver can finally gun the engine and show his passengers what an express can do.

To capture the full experience it is necessary to throw open the carriage window and, heeding the warning sign *non sporgersi dalla finestra, pericolo di decapitazione* (do not lean out of the window – danger of decapitation), position yourself with a good forward view to Venice shimmering in the distance like a mirage above the azure waters of the lagoon gliding past at great speed. Unlike a mirage, however, Venice approaches with alarming rapidity and just as you begin the calculation for the breaking distance for several thousand tons of Italian rolling stock travelling at great speed, the driver applies the breaks using the 'just in time' principle of train driving to ensure a smooth entrance into Santa Lucia station – a large elegant modernist building from the 1930s.

After struggling down onto Italy's incredibly low station platform with bags and cases, you enter the air-conditioned relief of the station concourse where the traveller can fortify themself with wine and *spaghetti alle vongole* from the station café. Then, finally, a moment you will never forget. Step out under the huge cantilever of the station canopy, whose modernist lines create a vista with the proportions of a cinema screen revealing a scene depicting the noise, colour and vitality of life as if in a movie by Roberto Rossellini. The Grand Canal is before you. Step into the picture – you have arrived in Venice.

The following examples show that the principles which make Venice work can be successfully applied to modern day cities to create arrival points, movement systems and enjoyable places just like Venice. Venice works; this book shows that modern cities can also work in the same way.

Opposite The richness of Venice lies beneath the public façade

Arriving in the City

Arriving in the City

First impressions count. City planners have recognised this for thousands of years. The Colossus of Rhodes, the triumphal arches in Rome, the Parthenon in Greece, were all designed to impress and amaze visitors and to establish in their mind that they had arrived in one of the world's great cities.

In more recent times, the dramatic sight of the Statue of Liberty or the grandeur of the Golden Gate Bridge told ship-borne travellers they were arriving somewhere special.

In the twenty-first century the ubiquity of the mass media makes it more difficult to surprise or delight travellers, but it can be done.

Railway stations, bus terminals and airports can be a squalid and exhausting experience. They are often disordered, confusing and challenging. But they need not be.

Arrival points are a shop window to the city. Their design should reflect civic aspiration whilst meeting transport needs. They succeed by recognising what travellers need in terms of information and comfort and what cities really want in terms of image projection.

The examples that follow – whether large or small: famous or little-known – show arrival experiences at their best. Be they of grand design or intimate proportion, they set a positive tone for the city they serve.

Opposite *The Golden Gate – first impressions count*

*The terminal building is elegant, yet understated, using traditional
Norwegian materials, such as wood, glass and stone*

Gardermoen Airport, Oslo

Norway

The Norwegian Parliament's mission was to construct not only a new airport, but a gateway that would become a part of the Norwegian landscape and promote travel to the country through simplicity, functionality, accessibility, and an overall sense of timeliness. The result is one of the best examples of a modern arrival point that creates a positive and lasting impression.

Opened in 1998, Oslo Gardermoen Airport creates a memorable point of arrival to the city. It portrays an image of quality, efficiency and attention to detail. For many people, the airport will be their first impression of the country and the overall impact is stunning, reflecting positively both on Oslo and Norway as a whole.

The airport is designed to handle 17 million passengers per year and will do so in an environmentally sustainable way. This is seen in the choice of materials and the design of details and communications systems.

The terminal building uses traditional Norwegian materials: wood, glass and stone. The overall impression is of quality, simplicity and beauty. Norwegian art is seen in many of the details.

The building feels light and airy helped by the extensive use of glass. However, internal lighting is also well designed to cope with the long, dark, Nordic winter nights.

A careful and deliberate design strategy has ensured visual consistency in the architecture, furnishings, fittings and communications

Gardermoen Airport is one of the best illustrations of a modern arrival
point that creates a positive and lasting impression

Floor to ceiling windows provide light that penetrates the internal areas,
making the outside seem accessible from the inside, bringing the
Norwegian landscape to the traveller

Travelling can be very tiring and stressful so at arrival and departure points one needs to feel relaxed and comfortable. The incorporation of art helps achieve this and comes in many forms around the airport. For example, the glasswork on the bridges, the drinking fountains and moving sculptures in the arrivals area.

It is also a very functional arrival point. If you reach first floor level by car or bus, you walk across connecting bridges through a glass wall towards the check-in desks and departure area. All the time, because of the transparency of the building you feel you are being drawn to the aircraft awaiting you. Often airports can be stressful and confusing; by opening out the terminal and bringing airside and landside close together, the process of negotiating the airport has been made easy and enjoyable.

Arriving passengers experience the same design principles. They are separated vertically from departing passengers; each being transported to their destinations on efficient travelators. If you need to rest for a short while, the seats provided are of a wonderful quality and design using leather, wood and steel; echoing again the natural resources of Norway.

It is vital that any airport is well connected to the rest of the transport systems. Gardermoen satisfies this criterion well. It has to because over 40,000 people will travel to and from the airport every day. This is achieved by providing connections with road, bus, rail and car parking that are of a standard not seen before in Norway. Motorways and key main roads have been widened on the approaches to the airport and over 10,000 dedicated parking spaces have been created. Automated signs even indicate the route to the nearest space or disabled parking bay.

The airport railway station is integrated with the terminal building and a new high-speed railway connects to central Oslo. Many other train services link the outer reaches of Norway with this excellent transport interchange.

Efficient and regular bus services from outside the terminal building connect this international gateway to the rest of the country. The airport is able to offer, therefore, a comprehensive travel service to many areas of Norway.

Gardermoen Airport provides, for many passengers, their first experience of Norway. It is a memorable experience, reflecting the art, science and skills of Oslo and Norway. This impressive point of arrival is simple and easy to follow, whilst at the same time ensuring an enjoyable travel experience. It is a great credit to all those who played a part in its provision.

The enclosed, arched design offers passengers a sense of security about their impending journey

The New TGV Méditerranée Stations

France

TGV stations prepare travellers for the idea that they are about to embark upon an enjoyable railway journey. They predispose people to feel positive about the train as a means of transport. As arrival points they project a high quality image, which reflects on their cities and surrounding areas. The design philosophy for each is different, responding to the needs of the local climate, providing a unique arrival point in harmony with the local landscape.

To travel on the TGV is to experience rail travel at its best. The journey from Lille to Marseilles takes around four hours. As one rides through the French countryside at speeds of up to 300kph, there is hardly a tremor on the surface of the coffee.

Yet it is the new arrival points on the TGV Meditérranée, opened in 2001, which truly take your breath away. To arrive at Valence, Avignon and Aix-en-

Provence is to land in an oasis of great design; a place which speaks of quality and impact. It immediately translates into the message that 'I want to be here' and the associated towns are special places to visit. This is the power of compelling design of transport facilities.

The platform is reminiscent of a seaside boardwalk with faraway views of the papal palace and Avignon

*On arriving in Valence, the TGV has to slip beneath other tracks into a
trench 7 metres below the surface*

The entire space is reserved for seeing and moving, key elements of a modern arrival point

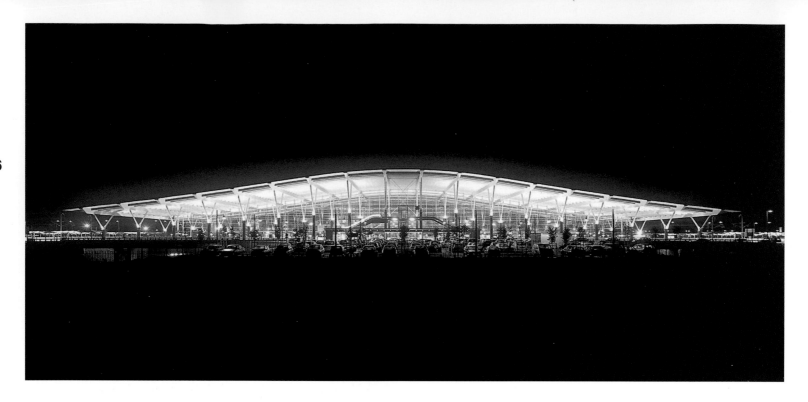

The vast metal canopy with its gentle curve echoes the silhouette of the nearby mountains

The driving force behind the success of these arrival points is architect Jean-Marie Duthilleul. He played no part in planning routes or designing trains, but concentrated purely on the space passengers experience as they board or alight the trains – the in-between places where people pass each other in transit, where they arrive and where they leave.

In choosing to head an SNCF construction department, Jean-Marie Duthilleul recognised the opportunity that it gave to rethink the design of railway stations. Rather than create buildings, he focused on the crowds who hurry through the stations onto the platforms. The emotions that are present in the embracing and good-byes, the waiting, the jostling; he saw the stations as great theatres of life. This is what inspired his designs.

VALENCE

Valence station looms up on the outskirts of the city like a vast slab of glass straddling the line. The design described a horizontal between the three local mountain ranges of Drome, Ardeche and Vercors. Anything that risked intrusion into the mountain landscape was deemed unacceptable

On arriving in Valence, the TGV slips beneath other tracks into a trench 7 metres below the surface. The platform becomes a vast 300-metre-long gallery protected by a flat roof 15 metres above it.

The trench is criss-crossed with walkways, escalators, metal tubes and cables lit by reflected light from the glass façade, providing a bright and airy environment for the traveller. There is always something to look at. The station is designed to draw the eye to the distant blue, Vercors hills on the horizon. The traveller's eye enjoys the orchards and tulip trees that conceal the car parks and encircle the station to the hills beyond.

The structure of the station is as arachnidan as possible. Everything stems from the two walls flanking the TGV. Just as the planes are never horizontal the structure has no verticals. The entire space is reserved for seeing and moving; key elements of modern arrival point design.

Once inside the station there's a six-metre difference in height at either end of the 200-metre concourse, which is suspended in mid-air. At one end is the regional station (TER) and at the other end the TGV; but both are on the same concourse. From the TGV station passengers can see the Vercors Mountains and at TER they can gaze out to the distant horizon. It is a station suspended in space, creating the impression of floating in the landscape.

AVIGNON

The area surrounding Avignon station is symmetrically landscaped and, like Valence, planted with rows of tulip trees. In contrast to Valence, the Avignon tracks are above ground with the station on a lower level.

Avignon station is built on flat land at the confluence of the Rhone and Durance Rivers. It cannot be seen in its entirety from any one direction. Its south face looks like a large pebble that has been pulled out of shape. The glazed façade to the northern side starts on the same level as the trains, but is half the height of the southern face. The platform is reminiscent of a seaside boardwalk with far-away views of the papal palace and Avignon.

It is a concept of great beauty, which is flooded by light and exudes quality and good design. Every detail shows that great thought and care have been put into the structure. The design reflects the fact that passengers had to be protected from the Mistral wind. Its shield-like faces ward off the wind from the north and the south; the glass face protects from the wind and collects light – its slatted face protecting from the sun. These walls are expressed in a slow curve, which extends the central area to accommodate the numbers of people, diminishing towards either end. It is a delight to experience this arrival point and a perfect anticipation to the town of Avignon.

AIX-EN-PROVENCE

One station further down the line from Avignon is Aix-en-Provence. Built on the Arbois plateau, just above the city of Vitrolles, it stands in the midst of a beautiful landscape, but does not embarrass. The station straddles the main road from Aix-en-Provence to Mirignane airport.

The concourse and station roof are asymmetrical. To ward off heat and bright sunshine, the south façade is covered in moveable slats of wood; the only obstacle to the panoramic view, revealed from the huge, partially glazed space. A walkway runs from one end of the station to the other above the tracks and a terrace looks out onto Mont Sainte-Victoire.

The station was designed as a place for contemplation, where people 'could stroll halfway between heaven and earth, town and nature, movement and stability'. Its relationship with the surrounding landscape is more explicit than the other two stations, hence the idea of the vast metal canopy with a gentle curve mirrors the silhouette of the nearby mountains. It is a concourse that always provides a view, both internally and externally.

These three stations are perfect examples of arrival points that delight the visitor and create an impressive, symbolic advertisement for the towns they introduce. They also show how design, even for railways, can be functional, yet inspire and excite. They care and display compassion for the surrounding countryside and love for their railway, their towns and their country.

Design has captured the immediacy of travel and made the outside world appear accessible from inside

Chek Lap Kok Airport

Hong Kong

The airport succeeds in bringing the departing passenger close to the plane and the arriving passenger close to the city. The whole design is intended to reduce the feeling of an airport as a place where passengers are forced to spend time, into an enjoyable aspect of transition.

Chek Lap Kok Airport extends a concept pioneered by famed British architect Lord Foster. It is characterised by a lightweight roof, natural lighting and integration of baggage handling, environmental services and transportation all beneath the main concourse. With its uncluttered spaces, bathed in natural reflected light, it forms a spectacular gateway to the city.

Airports may not be the equivalent of the traditional city square with all its excitement and variety, but they are a very important component of public life for many countries, even some of the poorest. They set the tone for the city and are a measure of status. This is particularly true in East Asia where other airports, such as Osaka in Japan, have followed the same philosophy as Hong Kong.

Until recently, Hong Kong's air traffic was managed by Kai Tak Airport, which was congested and on limited land. Its only runway was on the banks

An island in the Hong Kong archipelago was levelled and land reclaimed to provide for runways and a visually exciting passenger terminal

Above *Passengers are able to view the aircraft from the passenger lounge –
capturing a sense of immediacy*
Opposite *Uncluttered spaces bathed in reflected natural light form a spectacular
gateway to the city*

of the Kowloon River opposite Hong Kong Island and right in the middle of a residential area. Although landing between skyscrapers was spectacular for passengers, it was extremely difficult for pilots!

A hilly island in the Hong Kong archipelago was levelled and land reclaimed to provide the surface for new runways and a passenger terminal, that would be a visually exciting introduction to Hong Kong and southern China.

The basis of Foster's design reflects his experience in America in his early years. The airports he worked on were small airports where passengers arriving by car could immediately see the aeroplanes that would connect them to the rest of the world. The design of Chek Lap Kok tries to capture this immediacy.

The essential movement pattern of Chek Lap Kok is very simple. Arriving at the Ground Transportation Centre on the east side, departing passengers are conveyed by bridges across a void where people below can be seen arriving and being welcomed by friends and family.

The entire space is covered by parallel roof vaults, curving slightly upwards in the direction of travel, drawing the passenger forwards.

The four-level Ground Transportation Centre houses the airport express trains and an extensive public transport interchange with facilities for taxis, buses, tour coaches, hotel limousines and private cars. It provides a fast and effective connection throughout Hong Kong and the region.

The airport is one of 10 related transport infrastructure projects undertaken in Hong Kong. These include 34km of expressways and new rail links, two major bridges, two tunnels connecting the airport to the city centre, and an express rail link between the airport and central Hong Kong. The airport is extremely well connected to the city and its hinterland, an essential component of good continuity in design.

The visual principles of being drawn from ground transportation to aircraft are maintained throughout the terminal design.

Arriving and departing passengers can be moved swiftly from even the furthermost gates in about 70 seconds

The space is covered by parallel roof vaults which swoop upwards in the direction of travel, drawing passengers forward

Arriving and departing passengers never meet but they can see each other from bridges

Passengers are able to view the aircraft from the departure hall. As they keep moving towards the aircraft they see the jagged blue outline of the Lantau Mountains and South China Sea through glass walls that give a panoramic view.

At Chek Lap Kok passengers always know where they are. The shape of the roof draws the arriving passengers across the slender bridges of the main void and past the check-in islands to the east hall, which the designers claim is the largest single international retail space in the world. If an airport can be likened to a city then this is its market place.

Arrivals are in an exact reverse pattern to departures, but a floor below. Arriving and departing passengers never meet, but they can see each other from the bridges. Over three kilometres of moving walkways and travelators swiftly transport arriving and departing passengers from the furthest gates in about 70 seconds.

It is not surprising that Chek Lap Kok has won the coveted title of 'Airport of the Year' for two consecutive years. It is functional, practical and beautiful. It determines the highest standards of service and convenience for passengers; the result is world class in every respect. It provides a memorable arrival point and enjoyable place of transition, leaving the passenger with a lasting and favourable impression of the city and East Asia.

Bus to rail is made swift and accessible
Detailed information makes transport transitions much easier

Translink Interchange, Bangor/Belfast
Northern Ireland

Passengers often experience an aversion to changing modes of transport. It feels complex and time-consuming, but the Bangor/Belfast interchange shows how even a small-scale centre can be designed in such a way to make the transition painless and, indeed, enjoyable.

Not all effective arrival points are on a grand scale; the Translink Interchange in Bangor, just outside Belfast, is an impressive example of how smaller urban areas can apply the same principles to great effect.

The architect's brief was simple: to design a state-of-the-art, user-friendly transport centre that would enable smooth transitions between bus, rail and the private car. This was to be the first of its kind in Northern Ireland since the bus and rail companies were integrated in 1995.

The result is striking, conveying a dynamic and forward-looking image in keeping with the new millennium. The building was planned to integrate with its urban environment, yet at the same time to make a modern and confident statement. It provides a feeling of comfort and quality, which enhances both the image of public transport as well as the surrounding area.

Human scale architecture

Open design and transparency lift travellers' spirits

The nautical design of the building makes dramatic use of glass and steel in its construction. The curved wave profile of the roof canopy, together with the free flowing cable-stayed structure and the transparency of the building, were designed to pick up and reflect the proximity of the sea.

It is a pleasure to enter the bright modern concourse by the main entrance, after crossing the new paved square in front of the building. It feels a nice place to be. The square is also accessible as a drop-off point for passengers and deliveries.

Inside the double-height concourse, the most striking feature is its transparency. From the first level, a wide stairway with curving steel and glass balustrades combines with the main stairway, the glass lift and escalator to provide access to the upper level. The impression created is of a kind of modern day amphitheatre.

To the front of the building a circular viewing area overlooks the concourse below and a series of windows offers views of the sea. The lower level includes shops, toilets, multi-accessible payphones, seating and information displays, and Translink's integrated bus and rail ticket office. Special station 'hosts' have also been appointed to ensure that customers receive the best possible service.

The twelve new bus stands are located along the Abbey Street side of the development. There is an external PA system, clear signage and comfortable passenger seating. A ramp links the bus stands directly to the rail platforms.

The flowing steel canopies, built between mast-like supports, cover the railway platforms and make waiting time more pleasant. Large blue polished tiles, in the company colour, line the walls and match the blue of the steel handrails inside the concourse.

Finally, 100 park and ride spaces have been provided within a new car park opposite the complex to help commuters switch to public transport for the final leg of their journey into the City of Belfast.

The interchange at Bangor is well designed, inspirational and lifts the image of public transport and the surrounding area. It is a pleasure to use and shows that even local, small-scale places can apply the principles behind the great modern arrival points in the world. It brings these principles within the grasp of all.

Nils Ericson Bus Station, Gothenburg

Sweden

The bus may often be seen as a humble form of transport, but dramatic and attractive bus stations can improve its whole image. The Nils Ericson Terminal is sensitively designed to reflect the human scale and provides an exciting place to be.

The conventional image of the bus station reflects that of the bus. It is generally thought of as a lower standard of travel and bus stations are not expected to be pleasant places; two components of a mutually reinforcing negative image.

This does not have to be. It is refreshing to find an example of a bus station that is not only a pleasant place to be in, but also a significant piece of architecture that transforms the conventional view and is a quality symbol of the city it serves. It demonstrates that it is possible to create a stimulating

arrival and departure point, which enhances the image of the bus.

The architect for the terminal was Niels Torp and his winning design has a bold and simple concept. A long, glazed gallery stretches north from the older Gothic-style

The use of warm, natural materials helps to introduce the human feel
Opposite *Light wood seating and indoor trees compliment the structure*

railway station; it interfaces with both heavy rail and the tram so that all land-based forms of transport meet at the terminal.

The basic design is similar to the Waterloo Channel Tunnel Terminus in London but the Gothenburg building is simpler because of its situation and requirements.

However, unlike the train terminal, Gothenburg's bus station has to be sealed from the elements. Nothing is underground; all activities take place at the same level. Travellers wait in a glazed area, protected from the Gothenburg climate, which can be harsh: wet, windy and cold in the winter and hot in summer.

The design of the roof both maximises daylight and acts to spread artificial light, giving a comfortable level of lighting at all times of the day and in all seasons. This is achieved through attention to the design detail.

One of the design objectives was to give the significant length of the building a sense of human scale and place. The shops are grouped in clusters around the three eastern entrances, which lead to the car park and taxi set-down area. The aim is to make the transition into the large glazed area as agreeable and welcoming as possible. A long and almost freestanding canopy of glass and steel shelters passengers from the weather and covers the shops making it practical as well as beautiful. The clever use of warm, natural materials, such as wood, helps to introduce a human feel.

The entrance gates to the buses are similarly made in traditional Scandinavian material: solid and welcoming wood, similar to the structure of the shops opposite. Light wood seating and large indoor trees enhance the structure and informally break up the bright gallery area.

One of the difficulties of modern public transport interchange design is to create a terminal that protects passengers from the past, unpleasant aspects of these places but avoids making them unattractive, bland and boring. The Nils Ericson building has achieved the former and avoided the latter. It is a terminal that protects, is functional and provides a place that is comfortable and pleasing.

Nils Ericson shows that it is possible to provide an arrival point that creates dramatic impact and high architectural quality, whilst being functional and comfortable and, to complete the picture, is a well-designed bus station too!

Opposite Nils Ericson is a significant piece of architecture that transforms the traditional view of a bus station

Grand Central Station, New York

USA

The renaissance of Grand Central Station is not just a story of the immediate transport hub, but of reinvigorating many aspects of the city around it. A point of entry and departure cannot simply be limited to the station itself. In some ways this is the success story of an organisational idea – the Grand Central Partnership.

One of the great, historic arrival points in the world is New York's Grand Central Station, transport grandeur that recalls the great days of train travel. Tragically, over the years time took its toll on the station. However, in early

1984 the Mobil Corporation produced a short video for the mayor of New York, which told the shocking story of how this once great station had declined.

The video showed all the negative aspects of the station: the homelessness, crime, litter and poor maintenance. It compared this state of affairs with the plush offices of some of the Fortune 500 companies. This video shocked the city authority and caused it to act to rectify the situation. Over the coming years they demonstrated how a great arrival point can become the focus for community regeneration around it.

Opposite *Central to the project was the concept of a pedestrian network that welcomed people and caused them to linger and enjoy the area*

Right *Original features were restored to their former glory*
Opposite *The objective was to recreate a living, vibrant community around the station*

In 1985, the Grand Central Partnership (GCP) was formed as a direct response to the Mobil video and complaints from other tenants and owners. GCP is a coalition of property owners, tenants and city officials whose aim is to dramatically upgrade the services and infrastructure within a fifty-block area bounded by Fifth Avenue, 48th Street, Second Avenue and 39th Street. The Mayor fully backed GCP by pledging to maintain the city's current level of services and lending his full support to GCP's plans. An effective public/private partnership model!

In July 1986 the GCP selected Benjamin Thompson and Associates, architects and planners, to study the area and propose physical changes and capital improvements to revitalise the district's street environment. The central objective of their plan was to recreate a living, vibrant community around the station. They identified all the problems and offered solutions which were practical and deliverable. They wanted to provide an environment where people would want to stay and enjoy the area. In September 1987 they proposed a five year master plan which included a list of actions and a handbook of design details. Within these ideas were innovative and exciting concepts like creating a boulevard of light on 42nd Street with street furniture specially designed to complement the idea.

Less than a year after the master plan was published the city gave the necessary approval, levied a special local tax and returned the resulting funds to GCP. To oversee the capital projects they chose Arthur Rosenblatt, former vice-president for architecture and planning at the Metropolitan Museum of Art.

One key aspect was that early results were seen; this was important to the project. These early wins included lights shining on the roof of the station and new, historic lamp posts on the Pershing Square viaduct. These were the first steps in restoring the original 1919 viaduct as part of the new Pershing Square which extended the full width of Park Avenue from 42nd Street to 40th Street. The

arches were used to provide glass-fronted cafés and other shops designed to serve the park and open a vista eastward from the Phillip Morris building to Witney Museum.

Central to the project was the concept of a pedestrian network that welcomed people, surrounded them with a safe and pleasant environment and caused them to linger and enjoy the area. It promoted life and vibrancy and was fundamental to the successful economy of the area. Within this concept were embedded a number of key aspects.

The first was to provide a system of pedestrian routes that were free of obstructions as much as possible. Street corners were cleared of clutter and repaved. The routes connected to traffic signal crossings and varying texture was used to guide people.

Secondly, planting and lighting were introduced. Trees were introduced in clusters on the street and at intersections. Lighting was placed on trees, and discreetly at ground level on storefronts, stairs and other street buildings and points of interest.

A new signing system was installed to help orientate people in an easily understood way. New street furniture was designed and kiosks were improved in quality, both in terms of their design and the goods they sold.

The planners segregated the users of information and designed the signing and information flow specific to each of their needs. For example, specially placed signs with international symbols and distinctive colours and shapes were introduced for drivers, people searching for parking, public transport users and people walking.

Another important aspect of the project involved the shop and office façades. Design guidelines were produced to assist property owners, empty shops became showcases for art and workshops were held for the retailers.

Other management measures were also put in place, including security officers patrolling the area and working with the police; a team of white-suited street sweepers clean the area daily and a special team remove graffiti and fly-posting. A multi-service centre has been setup, offering hot meals, counselling, job training and housing placement services and there are visitor and special events services available.

One of the major problems to be faced in tackling a project such as this is the plethora of agencies involved; often all with different agendas. Rosenblatt overcame this problem by proposing that a few blocks be developed at a time to demonstrate the new concepts in the plan. This could then be rolled out to other areas of the city without going through the same process of agreement of all parties. He had learned the lessons from other places in the world that often the way to gain acceptance of change is to introduce it incrementally; with each increment being designed carefully, to avoid evoking mass protest of the interested parties. The city supported this view which also helped significantly.

This project has taken one of the world's greatest arrival points, which had sadly declined, and transformed it not only to its former grandeur but made it the centre of a new, living community in the heart of New York. This successful redevelopment shows that arrival-points can be a catalyst for the regeneration of surrounding areas and communities.

Yokohama Ferry Terminal

Japan

The traditional function of a port is to mark the boundary between the inhabitants of the city and the visitors arriving by sea. Ports are gateways into the city, neither part of the urban fabric nor part of the sea, but the intersection of the two. Yokohama Ferry Terminal provides a gateway that is unique and exciting.

The grand idea behind the Yokohama Ferry Terminal is that it is not just a building to process passengers, but a public place for both residents and passing travellers. The architects, Foreign Office Associates, created the whole building in a park, with an undulating wooden surface where people can picnic, stroll, watch the world go by, sunbathe and which plays host to all the other activities that happen in an urban park. A grand hall for theatre and public events sits at one end of the terminal. It really is part of city life.

All of this overlaps with the arrival and departure halls through interconnecting routes and a design that eliminates walls and stairs. Its decks curve upward and downward to enclose rooms where necessary and link with other levels. The terminal is a complex mass of movement and interchange between visitors and the city inhabitants. The design uses the opportunity of these exchanges to

Above *The architects created the whole building in a park, with an undulating wooden surface where people can stroll, picnic or sunbathe*
Opposite *Yokohama Ferry Terminal provides a gateway that is unique and exciting*

Smooth and continuous movement relates to the transition between land and sea

*The design exudes modernity, quality, excitement and the prospect of
something quite different*

create fluid and uninterrupted streams of movement. This smooth and continuous movement relates to the transition between land and sea.

This continuous sequence, rather than the usual abrupt transition, is achieved by stretching the duration of the arrival along the length of the pier. This extension of arrival establishes a gradual transition from the city and its landscapes to the sea and vice versa. It is, therefore, not a vertical separation but a horizontal line of space and time between city, garden and sea.

The transition occurs in two directions along the pier, the first from the sea into the city, which defines the port, and the second from the city to the water, which defines the garden. Upon disembarking from the sea, passengers pass through the arrival hall, which gradually transforms into the surface of the plaza. Likewise, the citizen approaches through an enclosed garden whose natural terrain blends into the surface of the sea. The design intermingles these two passages and gives the user the combined effect of a city space, an arrival space and a transportation interchange all in one.

The terminal building is built on the spot where, in 1859, Japan made its first trading connections with the West. The terminal is a combination of the global and the local, the stable and the transient. It is a town square, a place of exchange for the 21st century.

The scale of this project is interesting. When ships arrive, especially the great cruising liners, they tower over the terminal. Passengers will feel they are looking down on an elegant pier, which exudes good design, quality, excitement and the prospect of something quite different. It demonstrates that even port terminals can be interesting places and can project positively the all-important first impressions of a city.

Within the terminal the arrivals and departures hall is reminiscent of a 21st century version of a Gothic vault. The proportions could be daunting and uncomfortable. However, the effect is pleasing and comfortable through the sensitive and limited use of materials which give a wholeness to the space and connect to the city outside. The feeling one gets is of a relaxed and simple place; it is a large space but it does not overwhelm the visitor.

It is such a pleasure to see a city being bold and innovative and showing the world that passenger port terminals do not have to be somewhere to get out of as quickly as possible. They do not have to be dingy, oppressive spaces. Yokohama has provided a wonderful example of a great arrival point by sea. The designers have also provided an immediate and lasting impression of their city that visitors will never forget.

Opposite The terminal is a complex mass of movement and interchange between visitors and city inhabitants

Salamanca Train Station
Spain

Salamanca train station illustrates how the city can be brought into a transport interchange and an arrival point can be brought into the city. Centro Estacion de Salamanca is a transport hub that combines interchange with retail and food outlets and a sense of theatre.

Salamanca is a remarkable city; a city of narrow streets, wonderful churches and the oldest university in Spain. Lunch in the Plaza Mayor is one of the great experiences of cities in the world. It was therefore a considerable design challenge to integrate the development of the small, existing rail station with retail and entertainment uses, in addition to creating a new arrival point for the city.

The architects and urban designers RTKL were selected by Grupo Riofisa to design a 15,000m^2 retail and entertainment venue as an addition to the

train station. They were faced with a tight budget of around 1.4 million Euros and a challenge to create a new front door for visitors arriving in the city, a viable retail and entertainment venue and a landmark addition to the city's existing fabric.

The station sends the message of modernity, excitement, fun and quality

A transport hub that combines interchange with retail and food outlets
It is a shopping place, a meeting place and a place to watch the world go by

The design philosophy was to create a civic place on the street and shade it from the hot Spanish sun. The architects modestly extended the arrival sequence through the station to gain shop frontage and lined the path with convenience and necessity retail. Finally, they placed retail uses that would function as destinations, cinema and food outlets adjacent to the paths of passengers. The spaces created are high and light and the murals tell the history of rail travel. A large clock reminds you of your train time!

The building is a mix of traditional and modern materials. Most of the façade is clad in local stone, which ties the Paseo de la Estacion in with the surrounding buildings. The v-shaped, metal-clad columns in the forecourt support a blue blanket above. This blue blanket is made of glass-reinforced gypsum cast into a series of waves linking the public forecourt to the main mall.

But while this is a gateway and public amenity, it is also a shopping centre. An important principle underlying the provision of the shopping was that it should complement the local high street, not challenge it. What this means in practice is that the shops lining the frontage are convenience stores and necessity retailers. A small supermarket was added due to a local shortage of such a facility.

The designers worked closely and successfully with the local planners and the public within a culture that understands and enjoys good design. It is a culture that appreciates how good design contributes not only to the environment and quality of life, but also to the economy, as more people spend more time in the area sampling its ambience and buying the services on offer.

The concept of the Salamanca rail station is an important one. It is a concept seen more and more around the world; using transportation terminals as much more than barren interchange points that passengers want to leave as soon as possible. They can be exciting places to be in. An arrival point can be a place that performs many functions and is a signpost to the city. People are realising that the arrival point, just like the front counter in any business, is the key to a positive first impression of the city. It sets the tone and projects a positive image of the city.

Salamanca train station sends the message of modernity, excitement, fun, quality and appreciation of fine things. It is also a hub of activity in the style of the past where many facets of the city meet. It is a shopping place, a meeting place, a place to watch the world go by and a place that complements the city around it.

The designers have shown how retail and transport interchange design can be combined to bring the city into a railway station and an arrival point into the city. Much can be learned from commercial retail design in this context. This example also shows the effect climate has on design and local culture. Transport and retail centres are now seen as opportunities to promote good architecture and urban design; to create positive images of the city. Salamanca train station is a great, modern example of this.

The ambience encourages people to spend more time in the area

Enjoying the City

Enjoying the City

People live in and visit cities for work and leisure. Cities that exist principally as political centres or business districts tend to be soulless and depressing. As night falls the office workers leave and they often revert to desolate urban wastelands.

Grand architecture and sweeping avenues may look imposing, but are not enough by themselves. The skill is to create an urban environment that feels human and generates a subtle sense of ownership and usable public space – a vital aspect of urban vitality.

The pubs of London, the pavement cafés of Paris and the urban beach in Brisbane, all reflect the demand of local people. They provide a meeting ground, a social centre, a place of entertainment and a vast array of cultural experiences. These authentic, local attractions are the key elements that draw tourists and locals alike.

City governments typically spearhead the creation of public spaces, museums, libraries and art galleries, whilst cinemas, theatres, shops and restaurants are the result of entrepreneurial activity. Great, exciting cities form out of these natural private/public partnerships.

People warm to cities when they find the environment sympathetic. An unexpected statue or sculpture, an open green space or trees by the side of the road – these delights make a city a pleasure to be in. As Professor Jan Gehl has said, a city should be like a good party – you just don't want to leave!

Small streets are festooned with geraniums and bougainvillea
Old town Marbella is maintained to a very high standard – there is no
graffiti or litter anywhere

Marbella Old Town

Spain

When faced with an old town that was inaccessible, damaged and without a soul, the merchants and professionals of Marbella knew something had to be done. Their 'Millennium Plan' was the catalyst in rescuing the ancient city centre and creating an oasis of pleasant streets and squares that work both economically and environmentally.

One of the most enjoyable city centres in the world is Old Town Marbella, Spain. The buildings are around 2,000 years old, but towards the end of the 20th century the area was in poor repair. Recent regeneration and management have now created a neighbourhood of astounding quality with a stunning public realm. It provides an excellent example of how older city centres can be sensitively improved and managed to create enjoyable and lived-in neighbourhoods appropriate to the 21st century.

In the 1980s Marbella citizens became aware that the changes happening were threatening the whole life and fabric of the city. They could see that these trends were going to cause damage to the environment and the economy of the city. Many areas had become inaccessible, damaged and without life. The historic city centre was dying economically and socially. Something had to be done.

The centre piece of the old town in the Plaza de Los Naranjos

Marbella is a popular coastal town attracting a large number of tourists to its modern beach front

In response, the 'Asociacion de Comerciantes y Profesionales del Casco Antiguo de Marbella' (ACPCAM) was formed, an association of merchants and professionals from the old town. The ACPCAM developed and presented to the city council an action plan that set out their understanding of the problems, their aims, ideas and solutions for the 2,000-year old city centre. At the core of their strategy were four plans: pedestrian priority; urban recovery; management and maintenance; and, finally, making utilities invisible.

The first plan deals with the pedestrianisation strategy, public car parks, residential parking and signage. The second, and perhaps the most important, dealt with the urban agreements to refurbish damaged areas, including the recovery of the Arab Castle, the Royal Hospital of San Juan de Dios and the Monastery of the Trinitarios.

The management and maintenance plan deals with the day-to-day cleaning and maintenance of the city centre. As a result, Marbella now has extremely efficient and effective cleansing services – there is no graffiti or litter anywhere. The plan also covers the entrances to the central area, the street decoration and furniture, the landscaping and the maintenance of the buildings around the squares.

The hiding of utilities is the latest plan to be implemented and deals with the removal from view of overhead cables (such as electricity and telephone). In the future all new wires and cables will be placed underground.

The plans had a budget of 15 million Euros, and enabled the renewal and rebuilding of an area of 27,000m^2 and provision of 500 new car spaces, all under municipal management and control. Approximately 7,000m^2 of vacant land were bought by the city council, urban agreements were delivered and subsidies received from the regional government and European Community.

The effect of these plans over the past decades has been remarkable. The quality of the pavement surfaces, comprising a mixture of materials and intricate mosaic stonework, is superb. The surface has been laid with great care – not one stone out of alignment nor any instance of substandard finish or reinstatement. The combination of modern refurbishment with ancient buildings is impressive and creates a network of streets and squares that engenders a feeling of comfort and enjoyment.

The centrepiece of the old town is the Plaza de Los Naranjos. The square is laid out with neatly trimmed hedging around the orange trees, an old stone fountain and a central statue of the king. Around the outside of a café area, stone seats are placed under the trees and the buildings have large earthenware pots with plants decorating their frontages.

Off the main square is a series of small streets festooned with geraniums and bougainvillea, showing up in bright contrast against the whitewash of the buildings. In every street the same standard of finish and maintenance is encountered. All the streets have busy shops, many of them selling high quality merchandise in keeping with the ambience of the area. No traffic is allowed so pedestrians can amble through the narrow streets in safety and comfort.

Marbella Old Town is a fine example of how to rescue an ancient city centre from the threats of traffic and the most destructive trends of modern living. The transformation is incredible as is the quality of design and finish. One of the most impressive aspects, which many cities fail to address adequately, is the very successful cleaning and maintenance regime.

The public and private agencies in Marbella have shown that it is possible to create a city centre that is a delight to be in, that lives in the age of the car and can still grow economically. The city is to be congratulated on its vision, commitment and strategy. We can learn a great deal from this example, especially how to care for the fabric of our cities year after year.

A lively precinct that is home to much of Brisbane's cultural offering

The South Bank, Brisbane

Australia

When a motorway cut off the city from its river on its North Bank, Brisbane rediscovered its urban roots by actively developing the previously blighted South Bank. It created a central area, mixed-use community beside a river, complete with steel arbour and artificial beach. It provides a wonderful contrast between the two river banks and a fine example of the best in city living.

There is no finer example of the rediscovery of a city than in South Bank, Brisbane. On the north side of the Brisbane River an urban motorway snakes its way along the bank cutting off the river from its city; a man-made barrier from the 1960s. But opposite is South Bank, a place to enjoy the city free

from the dangers of traffic, recapturing the environment a city centre can offer.

Brisbane is a vibrant, fast growing city of around 1.8 million people, located on Australia's Pacific coast. The use of the Brisbane River, which winds its way through the city, has been key to building the qualities of the new Brisbane, engendering a relaxed outdoors lifestyle in keeping with the ethos of Queensland.

South Bank was the stage for the World Expo '88; this event gave the starting point for the transformation of the area into a lively precinct and destination

South Bank recaptures the environment a city can offer

A man-made beach is within walking distance of the business district
South Bank's relaxed outdoor lifestyle is in keeping with the ethos of Queensland

that is home to much of Brisbane's cultural offering, with centres for arts, theatre, education, eating, residential, commercial, convention and entertainment activities.

Over 9 million people visit South Bank each year, with almost 5 million enjoying the delights of the lush 17-hectare Parkland that includes a white sandy beach and swimming lagoon, a river front promenade with cafés and restaurants, forest walks and water features. An award-winning sculptured steel arbour covered in bougainvillea provides a signature landmark feature, which ties all the various elements together.

The South Bank Corporation was established in 1989 and briefed to develop the former Expo '88 site and adjoining South Bank precinct. The Corporation sought commissions from five architecture practices to prepare an integrated development plan for South Bank Parklands. This opened only four years later in June 1992.

The main architectural feature of South Bank is the arbour, consisting of 403 curling tendril-like steel posts strung with wires supporting a massed canopy of flowers. A ribbon of yellow steel is suspended beneath the arbour and doubles as a shading device and weather shield. Rest points and disabled lift access to underground car parking are located along its length. At night the arbour is lit to highlight the individual posts and the pathway. The effect is stunning and creates a unique centrepiece to the area.

The man-made beach overlooks the river and the Central Business District. It comprises a clear lagoon, white sandy beaches, palm trees, rocky creeks and shady hollows thick with sub-tropical trees and plants. All of this is within walking distance of the offices of central Brisbane. It is an extraordinary experience to lie on the beach and look across the river to the bustle of downtown Brisbane. The beach is patrolled seven days a week by experienced lifeguards and is the subject of a rigorous cleaning programme.

South Bank has promoted Brisbane's city living in a very significant way. A $100 million residential, retail and commercial development is changing the face of the area. New, elegant apartment blocks, specialist retail shops and commercial offices are bringing fresh life to the city. People have rediscovered the advantages of living in a mixed-use community in the middle of the city and enjoy being surrounded by the academic and cultural quarters, the Parklands, the beach, restaurants, cafés and shops.

Grey Street has been recreated as a grand, tree-lined boulevard of shops, hotels, theatres, cinemas, restaurants, cafés, apartments and offices and has a huge car park underground serving its functions and activities. Little Stanley has become a cosmopolitan neighbourhood with fashionable eating houses open from early morning to late at night. It offers people a retail mix that is eclectic, new and inspiring. There is something for everyone.

Spanning the southern edge of South Bank and the Central Business District and the Botanical Gardens is the Goodwill Bridge. The bridge is restricted to pedestrians and cyclists and over 40,000 people use it each week. It provides an umbilical link between the centre and South Bank. A catamaran boat service, the Citycat, operates along the river and also joins the two sides together. It is an impressively quick and efficient method of getting around the city and is fun to use.

South Bank is a perfect example of rediscovering and enjoying city living; overcoming the severance caused by the motorway system on the other bank. Brisbane is the place to see the right and wrong way to enjoy a river setting by the city.

Copenhagen Squares and Spaces

Denmark

The experience from Copenhagen highlights the threat of change and how to overcome its dangers. Copenhagen reclaimed its city centre streets and squares from the car in small increments over many years. The success of each step prepared for the introduction of the next.

Copenhagen is one of the world's best examples of a city reclaiming public space for its people. Up until 1962, all the streets in the city were filled with traffic and parked cars. Old photographs of the city squares show them to have been largely inaccessible and a poor environment for pedestrians; great assets which could not be enjoyed.

In November 1962, Copenhagen's main street, Stroget, was the first to be

turned into a pedestrian area. This was hotly debated at the time, but the new street proved an immediate success. Many did not believe that a cold, northern European city could have pedestrian streets and squares, and outdoor cafés! However, Stroget proved to be the start of a remarkable transformation of the core of the city, from overcrowded traffic environment into a lively people-orientated centre.

Over a period of 34 years the traffic and parked cars have gradually been removed from the central area.

__Above__ Market stalls flourish in once car dominated streets
__Opposite__ Until 1962 all the streets of Copenhagen were filled with traffic and parked cars

Copenhagen is one of the world's best examples of a city reclaiming public space

Stroget has become a lively people-orientated centre

One-by-one the city squares have been reclaimed and turned into well-used people places where bars flourish and musicians play. The key to this success has been understanding the threat of rapid change and introducing the transformation gradually.

Each year a small number of parking spaces was removed, a street was pedestrianised or traffic reduced. In this way people and businesses could see and experience the change in small increments and were not threatened by it; instead they welcomed it. People had time to change their travel patterns and adjust to the new system.

Stroget has been renovated and upgraded several times since it was first pedestrianised. It is the main link in the pedestrian system, handling east-west connections across the city centre. It is the place to see and be seen; the major city promenade. Walking down the street people will encounter great shops and entertainers of all descriptions. The street is full of city life, which in turn means a healthy economy.

After the success of Stroget, it seemed only natural to continue by closing the street of Fiolstraede to traffic. It was only eight metres wide and provided a north-south connection, linking the key public transport node of Norreport to the central part of Stroget. This street is unique as it is busy throughout the year. It lies in the middle of the university quarter, so when the tourists leave at the end of the

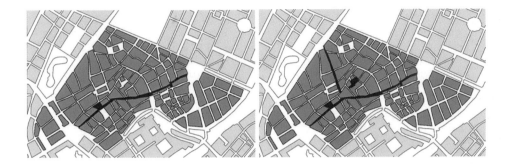

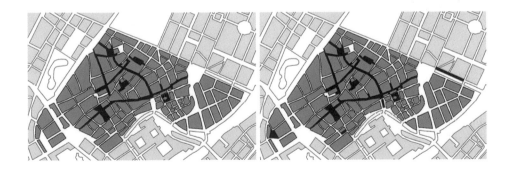

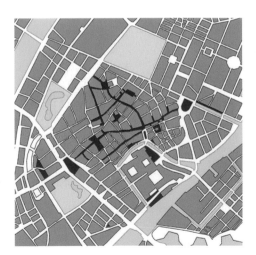

The green areas represent the pedestrianised streets implemented gradually since 1962

Nyhavn was cleared of cars in 1980 and has become one of
Copenhagen's most popular destinations

summer, the students arrive. This kind of mix of activities throughout the day and year is necessary for a successful city centre.

Following the success of the original streets, more were reclaimed each year. In 1973, pedestrian routes between key shopping areas and public transport interchange points were created. This also marked the beginning of a new phase of development for the next 20 years: reclaiming Copenhagen's squares from traffic and parked cars.

Today, Gammeltorv and Nytorv constitute one space, but they were originally two squares, separated by the old town hall. This double square, stretching across the path of Stroget, has always been one of the most important spaces in the city. Until 1962, the entire space was a huge car park, but since then it has gradually been turned into one of the world's great squares. Gammeltorv is popular and well used all year round. People like to relax near the famous Caritas Fountain and watch people going past on Stroget. Nytorv is quieter, but still provides the backdrop for several outdoor cafés during the summer months.

Many of the centre's smaller squares have also been reclaimed and provide peaceful havens for coffee and a rest. Grabrodretorv was the first of these smaller squares to be reclaimed in 1968. Dominated by a solitary plane tree this square, with its renewed

cobblestones and new fountain by Soren Georg Jensen, soon became one of the finest and most popular squares in the city. The square has an abundance of cafés and restaurants and is well used throughout the year.

Nyhavn is one of the greatest transformations in Copenhagen city centre. It used to be a busy part of Copenhagen harbour and a favourite pub-crawl for seamen. As harbour activities dwindled, Nyhavn became a car park. However, in 1980, the area was cleared of cars and turned into a pedestrian area. The location is perfect as it is a south facing quayside lined with old sailing ships. From the first days of early spring until late October, the place is now filled to capacity with people promenading or taking refreshments in the many cafés and restaurants.

Professor Jan Gehl, of Copenhagen Royal Academy, has said that if we design our cities to 'be loved by their citizens', then 'visitors will come and love them too'. He talks of city centres being abandoned, invaded by the car and finally being reconquered. Copenhagen in general, and Nyhavn in particular, are perfect examples of this process. It demonstrates that when we get the process right, the economy and the environment both benefit, and people enjoy an improved quality of life.

The Marketplace is Boston's central meeting place and attracts over 12 million people a year

Faneuil Hall Marketplace, Boston

USA

Faneuil Hall Marketplace in Boston has transformed historic buildings and brought them back to life and relevance in the 21st century. Its success is due to the vision of the developers and the combination of retail development and urban conservation.

Boston is a great city for people to enjoy. Situated on the east coast of the USA, Boston is arguably the most European of American cities. It is a walking city, well known for its Freedom Trail, a line around the centre, which will take you past many of Boston's historic landmarks; some of them unexpected like Old Mother Hubbard's grave. Yes, she did exist and lived in Boston. The central area is compact and clusters around a central park where it is possible to sit and relax or glide on the lake in one of Boston's famous swan boats. The historic Beacon Hill, with its cobbled streets is a short walk away, as is the waterfront.

It is the waterfront, more than any other area, which captures the people-orientated atmosphere of Boston. Since the 1960s Boston has been transforming its waterfront into an exciting and vibrant area, which people can enjoy. Central to this regeneration process was the creation of the Faneuil Hall Marketplace.

The Marketplace combines the glories of the past with the tranquillity of the

Quincy Market was designed in the Greek Revival style and named after the Boston Mayor Josiah Quincy

The public spaces are well designed and teem with activity

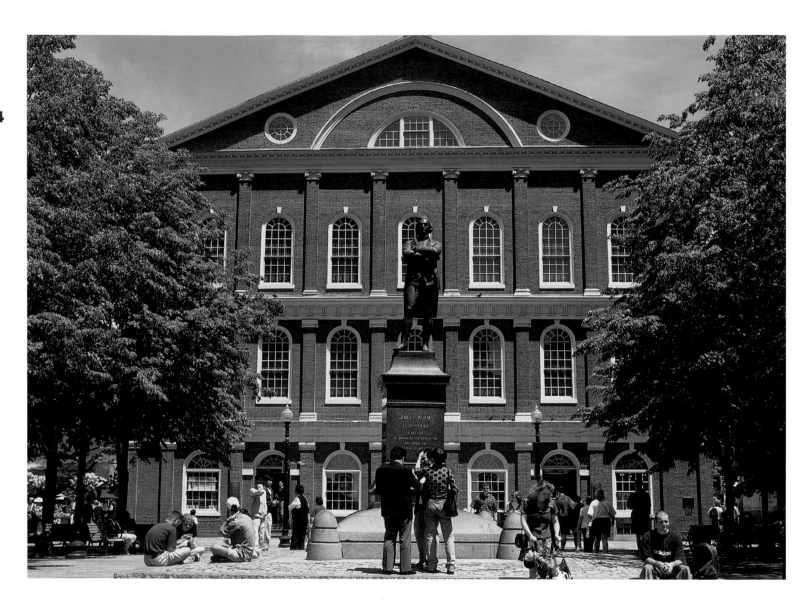

Peter Faneuil built the hall as a gift to the city in 1742

present. It comprises three restored 19th century buildings which combine historic, classical architecture with some modern additions. The public spaces are well designed and teem with activity from street performers to people sitting and enjoying the city buzz. It is an excellent example of the adaptive use of historic buildings. The development enhances their historic nature, bringing them back to life, and adding modern retail activity to attract people. It is the perfect example of urban conservation and modern retailing co-existing.

Faneuil Hall Marketplace was part of a large urban renewal project in the 1960s. The main square has government and state offices on two sides, providing office workers during the day and early evening for the shops, cafés, bars and restaurants. Faneuil Hall Marketplace, an old wholesale food market, was redeveloped in the 1970s and now forms the centrepiece of the development. The third side saw demolition of old warehouses to open up the waterfront and create a park and a hotel. This was completed in the 1980s. The fourth side houses buildings related to the city's financial community and this again brings life to the area during the day and early evening. At night many residents and visitors come to savour the atmosphere and to sample the food, drink, shopping and entertainment on offer.

All of this development has created a wonderful mixed-use area in the heart of the city, which buzzes throughout the day because of the services it offers and the critical mass and mix of people within walking distance. The Marketplace has over 70 shops, there are 14 full-service restaurants, 40 food stalls and Boston's most popular comedy nightclub. It is a great example of a living city centre. This 'festival marketplace concept', which Boston pioneered, has been widely adopted elsewhere, specifically in New York and Baltimore.

The history of the area gives it a special atmosphere; it has a very significant place in Boston's story. Boston's wealthiest merchant, Peter Faneuil, built Faneuil Hall as a gift to the city in 1742. The building was host to merchants, fishermen and meat and produce sellers and provided a platform for the country's most famous orators. It is where colonists first protested the Sugar Act in 1764 and established the doctrine of 'no taxation without representation'. Samuel Adams rallied the citizens of Boston to the cause of independence from Great Britain, and George Washington toasted the nation on its first birthday. Many famous speakers have graced the building, including Edward Kennedy and Bill Clinton. Its nickname of 'the cradle of liberty' shows it is well loved throughout the USA.

In 1826 Faneuil Hall was expanded to include Quincy Market, which was designed in the Greek Revival style and named after the Boston Mayor Josiah Quincy. The Market remained a vital business hub through the 1800s but by the mid-1900s it had fallen into disrepair and stood empty. It was due to be demolished but was saved by a committed group of Bostonians in the 1970s. Through the vision of Jim Rouse, head of the Rouse Company, architect Benjamin Thompson and Mayor Kevin White, the dilapidated structures were revitalised, transforming the face of downtown Boston.

Through the vision of these people we are now able to enjoy one of the world's greatest city experiences. Faneuil Marketplace, as it is now known, is Boston's central meeting place. It attracts over 12 million people a year; 140 million since 1976. A second renovation effort is underway to create additional restaurant space, increase outdoor seating and improve pedestrian walkways. The removal of the elevated motorway, which was built between the market place and the waterfront, further strengthened the pedestrian link to the sea.

In a poll published in *Landscape Architecture* in the 1980s, the two most important landscape architectural works in the previous 10 years were Freeway Park Seattle and Faneuil Hall Marketplace in Boston. Faneuil Hall set the agenda for urban design and renewal in Boston and, to a great extent, for the whole of the USA.

Faneuil Hall Marketplace really is a place to enjoy, and while you are there make sure to order Boston's famous Cajun style blue fish and then your experience will be truly complete.

Toronto Mall
Canada

A shopping mall in Toronto, designed by Santiago Calatrava, shows that we need not be limited in our ambition due to severe variations in weather. Enjoyable spaces can be created indoors in a protected environment, whilst maintaining a light and airy outdoor feeling.

Due to severe weather changes we are not always able to sit outside a café or stroll in leisurely fashion along the sidewalk and enjoy city life. It is encouraging therefore to see some cities overcoming these difficulties to create an enjoyable environment.

Toronto has very hot summers and very cold winters, frequently -20°C and below. The city needed therefore to create public space that could be air-

conditioned in summer and heated in winter. Many such malls are often cramped with low ceilings and almost devoid of natural light. Toronto has shown this need not be the case. It is possible to create light, airy and pleasant spaces that are protected from the extremes of climate.

Toronto's central area was always the life blood of the city, giving it a heart. However, as the effect of the late 20th century took hold, the central area lost its form and its vibrancy. The space that

Opposite *Enjoyable spaces can be created indoors*

remained was not of a human scale and difficult to utilise in a form that would be in harmony with the city's past and future. To address this problem a competition was held for invited artists, who were asked to submit ideas on transforming the space which was formed by a broad pedestrian passage that stretched in an east-west direction across the block from Bay Street to Yonge Street. The aim was to recapture the buzz of the city centre that had been lost.

What the city did not want was more of the same with some added civic art and a traditional, exposed square. The winning architect, Santiago Calatrava, acknowledged this and proposed a cathedral-like towering galleria reminiscent of Mengoni's great Galleria Vittorio Emanuele in Milan.

Calatrava's contemporary galleria works well. It is elegant, graceful and yet has the visible strength of engineering steel work. The structural design is not hidden; it is part of the dramatic effect the design creates. It is a design that relates directly to the city, linking into the surrounding street life and community. The quality of the finish and of the detail is very high and this is continued into the adjacent buildings and shops.

The project is centred on a long arcade that traverses the development and links two towers to a lower area at Yonge Street. The height of the arcade is of cathedral-like proportions rising to 27 metres and spanning 14 metres. The vaulting at either side reinforces that perception. The arcade ends in a covered square linking into a group of late 19th century commercial buildings. One of the buildings is the Darling and Curry's 1885 Bank of Montreal which survived the1904 fire. This joins the project to the city's past in a very tangible way. Restaurants and cafés at ground level give a life and vibrancy to the area throughout the day.

There is something magical about the space as one walks along its main arcade. Images of cascading water or tall palm trees lining a corridor of light come to mind. It is an urban boulevard comparable in an abstract way to the best European examples, yet it has been created in North America and indoors! It is a unique, extraordinary experience and one of delight.

Sometimes external influences stifle the creation of enjoyable spaces in city centres. Climate is one of those influences. Calatrava's mall in Toronto shows us that we can create enclosed city spaces that are exciting, enjoyable and elegant. We need not be limited by climate; indeed such limitations can stimulate the vision and imagination of people to the benefit of all. This Toronto mall is one to experience and enjoy.

Opposite *Calatrava's galleria works well. It is elegant, graceful and yet has the visible strength of engineering steel work*

Wall Murals

South Africa

A combination of art and advertising can provide a short-term contribution to urban regeneration for cities that do not have the budget to carry out major programmes. Not only can it raise revenue for the city's development projects, but also it lifts the public spirit and helps people see what the future could be like. It is a low-cost catalyst for longer-term regeneration.

Cities such as Buenos Aires, Toronto and Prague have all illustrated the beauty of art murals successfully, adding a sense of colour and vibrancy to drab, grey walls; however, no commercial revenue had actually been received for these projects.

In October 1993, a South African media company proposed the concept of wall murals for the first time to Johannesburg City Council. The idea provided the council with a platform for generating foreign exchange investment, employment for artisans and artists, income for the council, international exposure for the city on commercials utilising the murals and the promotion of local government and private enterprise cooperating in a joint-venture aesthetically improving the entrance to Johannesburg.

Environmental groups were enthusiastic about the project and claimed that the murals were one of the best examples of environmentally acceptable outdoor advertising. For the first time in South Africa the Ratepayers Association approved an outdoor advertising concept. The project was fully

Opposite *Covering the Munitoria building hid an eyesore and brought much needed revenue to the city*

supported by the Johannesburg Chamber of Commerce and Industry and the General Manager of the Outdoor Advertising Association.

The first three international companies to take up the project were British Airways, Dulux and Pepsi Cola. British Airways commissioned the Johannesburg Art Foundation to co-opt its students to design murals along an ethnic theme and the winning students were flown to London for the award ceremony for the chosen mural. Dulux utilised the idea of the new South African flag with the approval of the State President's Office. Pepsi Cola's design, expressing strong cultural community themes, was promoted through the Sowetan newspaper aimed at Sowetan artists. Soweto is South Africa's largest township. Since then Castle Larger, eTV News and McDonalds have also contributed to the murals.

In March 1997, the Munitoria building, the central municipal headquarters in Pretoria, burned down. The building was the pride of Pretoria and had hosted Archbishop Desmond Tutu's 'truth and re-conciliation commission' at the end of the apartheid years. The Munitoria fire was one of the largest commercial fires to have occurred in South Africa, with approximately 45,000m^2 of office space affected. As a result, monies were lost, rate statements were not delivered, building plans could not be approved and invaluable files were destroyed for ever.

While the insurance claim was the biggest commercial claim in South Africa, the City of Pretoria did not have the funds to redevelop the building. In April 1999, a local outdoor advertising company pro-posed a short-term regeneration solution to the eyesore that now spoiled Pretoria's landscape. This consisted of attaching 1,500 m^2 of illuminated vinyl onto the building, creating the largest billboard in the southern hemisphere. The advertising covered what had become a real eyesore and added considerable revenue to the city.

These large- and small-scale art projects lift spirits and give people a glimpse of what could happen in the future. They also help local people to feel good about their city and allow real com-munity involvement. They demonstrate a short-term, low-cost answer to urban regeneration and make the longer-term regener-ation of these areas easier.

Wall murals add a sense of colour and vibrancy
Small-scale projects can make local people feel good about their community

New Rondas, New Ramblas, Barcelona

Spain

The City of Barcelona has long recognised the importance, to the civic, tourist and economic life of the city, of an efficient and effective movement system for pedestrians and vehicles. In the last two decades, Barcelona has constructed a renowned system of public spaces and first class road networks. The new Ramblas and Rondas show how it is possible to balance space for pedestrian and vehicle movement to overcome traffic intrusion in order to connect historic public spaces into the old port, joining the sea to the city.

Since the 1980s, Barcelona has rightfully enjoyed a reputation as Europe's urban laboratory – a city turned to time and again by architects and urbanists for inspiration. Barcelona has achieved a radical transformation in its movement system and public spaces which have, in turn, greatly enhanced both enjoyment and accessibility of the city.

The new rondas were built in the 1990s as an orbital route to help free

the city from cross-town traffic. They take their name from the original rondas, a route around the old city constructed on the site of the former walls when they were demolished after the Peninsular War. Design of the new rondas employed many innovative and exciting engineering techniques. In the area between the old city and the old port,

Opposite *The world famous Ramblas run through the entirety of the old town into the regenerated port area*

Shops, cafes, market stalls and live entertainment make the Ramblas an exciting pedestrian walkway

New rondas were built to free the city from cross town traffic

the project faced a particular challenge to fit new roads into historic areas. At the same time, the new Olympic village was under construction to extend Barcelona's famous grid over former industrial land down to the Mediterranean coast. These parts of the route not only had to accommodate cross-town metropolitan traffic, but also the coastal motorway north to France and south to Valencia. Construction of the route in tunnel would have been extremely expensive and technically challenging and it would have denied travellers any glimpses of Barcelona city centre and the old port. In the end, an innovative engineering solution was adopted which combined open highway, parks, galleria and cut and cover to produce an exhilarating journey through the city which at the same time created the opportunity to lay out new parks and public spaces adjacent to and over the route together with vistas out to the city and the sea. The construction of the new rondas was an essential complement to the on-going programme of public spaces in the city – both key strands in the continuing programme of regeneration.

A particular challenge was faced in the section of route between the historic heart of the city and the old port. Here space was at even more of a premium than in the Olympic Village where the emerging urban plan was able to combine the needs of the new urban form with public space and highway engineering. At Moll de la Fusta, the old city waterfront, a large 12-lane highway severed the city from the port. In the competition winning solution, Ignacio de Sola Morales devised an ingenious solution: he separated traffic according to function and provided a dedicated road for each purpose – local traffic, cross town, motorway and port access all had dedicated carriageways separated from one another. Because traffic could no longer weave from one lane to another, capacity increased significantly. This solution not only used existing space more efficiently, but also created opportunity to win space for people in tree-lined boulevards and a new pedestrian *paseo* constructed over the route of the southbound motorway. The Moll de la Fusta project is an excellent example of a win–win urban project: much improved and enhanced public space for urban life together with greatly increased efficiency in the use of road space.

The public space programme in Barcelona is well known. It has proceeded through a number of phases starting with the opportunistic creation of small squares and parks when property values were low, and later moving on to refurbishment and renewal of existing spaces and squares and the creation of new and exciting spaces where opportunities presented themselves. One such example is the extension of the Ramblas out into the old port. The Barcelona Ramblas is a world famous example of historical opportunism. The word *rambla* is derived from the Arabic *raml* meaning a ditch. Over time the space evolved from its original purpose into a continuous sequence of broad streets or *ramblas* each with its own character reflecting the uses and markets which became established there: Rambla de les Flores – Street of the Flowers. This world famous street runs through the entirety of the old city down to the old port where, until recently, the coastal highway made it dangerous to cross. Completion of the Moll de la Fusta project made it possible to extend the Ramblas from the city out into the port to provide people with a pedestrian route into the newly regenerated port area with marina, shops and leisure facilities. The new structure provides an exciting opportunity to walk out to the regenerated peninsula of the old port across a structure which bridges the entrance to the marina. Pedestrians are provided with places to sit, sheltered from the wind by elegant glass screens, and watch activity in the marina and the port as they move between port attractions and the old city.

Barcelona has shown that it is important to recover space for people to enjoy the city on foot and to ensure that traffic can circulate efficiently. The city has successfully shown that efficient traffic circulation can also be enjoyable by ensuring that the driving experience is enhanced with stunning views of the city and its maritime setting.

Circular Quay and The Rocks, Sydney

Australia

The Rocks in Sydney is an example of the re-use of historic warehousing adapted to modern city living. Once a run-down and neglected area suffering from overcrowding and unsanitary conditions, it has become the hub of Sydney life loved by locals and visitors alike.

Circular Quay is the hub of Sydney Harbour, situated at a small inlet called Sydney Cove; the founding site for Sydney and Australia. Since the first European settlement, the Quay has been at the centre of Sydney's maritime life. Circular Quay is the 'hard-edge' along the water – a public space connecting transport, pedestrian and civic elements.

On the southern side of Circular Quay is a walkway that leads to Jorn Utzon's famed Sydney Opera House and the Royal Botanical Gardens; while on the northern side, a short walk along a waterside promenade takes you to

the Harbour Bridge and The Rocks, one of the older and more interesting parts of Sydney.

By 1840, The Rocks had grown into a thriving, if not seedy, port-side community. Ships from Europe, the Americas and Africa called into Sydney to exchange a variety of goods such as wool, sugar, whale oil and seal skins.

Historic brick and stone buildings dating back 150 years have been beautifully restored

*The street markets nestle under tent-like canopies, offering protection
from the sun and occasional rain*

Since the first European settlement, the Quay has been at the centre of Sydney's maritime life

Circular Quay is vibrant and fun and a location favoured for civic celebrations

The working-class residents of The Rocks lived in overcrowded and unsanitary conditions. The 20th century ushered in a greater danger: the bubonic plague. Authorities feared the disease would spread quickly through The Rocks. The government closed off the area for quarantine reasons and bought The Rocks for £1 million, citing public health concerns as the need to clean up the waterfront.

At first the government cleared only a few slums. But then entire streets were demolished to make way for the Sydney Harbour Bridge, completed in 1932, and later the Cahill expressway completed in 1962. The Rocks were thus severed from the city, but the neighbourhood, however, remained.

In the 1960s, the state government planned to clear the whole area and replace the remaining houses with modern skyscrapers, but the residents refused to leave. After many angry protests, the activists eventually prevailed in the mid-1970s. The government redirected its resources into preserving The Rocks, under the guidance of its newly established Sydney Cove Authority.

The emphasis over the next 25 years was on renovation and rejuvenation. Most of the historic brick and stone buildings – dating back 150 years – have been restored. Warehouses and terrace houses have been transformed into unique shops, galleries and restaurants. It is now a superbly regenerated area that buzzes with fun and activity.

The combination of the historic, restored buildings, the attractive shops and cafés, the street markets and entertainers and the human scale of the buildings makes this an exciting place to visit. It is a wonderful combination of the old and the new. Some of the merchandise is unusual and unique; a rare combination in our global marketplace.

Today, The Rocks is brimming with galleries containing Aboriginal to modern art, sculpture and photography, as well as ceramics and textiles. One of the streets, lined by historic, old stone buildings has a tent-like canopy spanning the street, with a market underneath. It offers protection from the sun and, on the odd occasion, the rain. Traffic is banned from these areas so pedestrians can wander in a safe and relaxed environment.

Fun is added in the form of Style Police. Actors dressed as traffic police, complete with revolving blue flashing lights on their helmets, give out tickets for pieces of clothing they feel do not conform to the style of The Rocks! The street bands and entertainers, and some of the stallholders also contribute to the fun.

Circular Quay connects all these elements by a waterside area that has been repaved and landscaped to create an attractive linear public promenade. It has services along its length orientated both to tourists as well as locals; fresh produce stands, restaurants, street performers and souvenir shops. It's also a prime place for the sun-worshippers who find that the concrete jungle of the CBD blocks their rays. The Quay is now a favoured site for civic celebrations. No matter where you are on the quay the Sydney Opera House and Sydney Harbour Bridge make their presence felt; a powerful and unique vista. Circular Quay is also a busy arrival point for all the harbour ferries and tours bringing a sense of vitality and busyness to the area.

Circular Quay and The Rocks are great examples of how derelict docks and former warehousing can be transformed into enjoyable, attractive city spaces able to generate income for the city's economy.

Its success lies in the combination of the historic setting and buildings, expertly restored, the quality of the retail offer and the environmental surroundings. The atmosphere is relaxed and friendly in a typically Australian way. The Rocks is an excellent example of re-using historic warehouses adapted to contemporary city centre living creating a combination of permanence and transient fun in the heart of the city.

Vancouver Downtown

Canada

Downtown Vancouver has been regenerated using sustainable development policies. Fundamental to the success of these policies is the planned density of housing in the area. This enables shops, community facilities and public transport to be supported; a critical mass of people has been established to make the community economically and environmentally viable.

Vancouver is a city set in a dramatic landscape, backed by the mountains and facing the sea. It is also a city that is projecting substantial growth and has been pioneering a range of projects to tackle this challenge in an innovative and sustainable way. Vancouver is in the midst of a boom in new housing in the city centre. The city is determined not to make the mistakes of the sixties and wants to build a city centre that is viable, beautiful, liveable and deliverable. Their strategy appears to be working.

The Expo '86 Fair site, on the North Shore of False Creek, was the catalyst that started the regeneration of the Downtown peninsula. East False

Creek and Downtown South followed Yale Town and Harbour Town. The planning projections estimated an additional 54,000 people moving into the downtown area of Vancouver; to date more than 30,000 people have made the transition. The effect of

Opposite *Vancouver is set in a dramatic landscape*

Most housing is in slim towers with three- or four-storey townhouse bases

Excellent transport is vital to the success of regeneration
Effective planning policy has ensured a continuous seawall walk

this critical mass of people is to make possible a range of services and transport that would otherwise be difficult to provide economically.

This means that Vancouver has created a community that is self-sufficient, whilst at the same time it has provided a great place to live. For example, it has meant that a local, high quality food store can operate without any car parking. The store survives because of the numbers of people, many of them high earners, living within walking distance. The store boasts a high quality café and ice cream shop and is busy throughout the day and evening.

Most of the housing is high rise with three- or four-storey townhouse bases. They have experimented, successfully, with European-type terraced housing, unusual for North American West Coast areas. Retail areas have become concentrated, creating a village feel. The city authorities encouraged developers to use the waterfront to create a continuous walkway along it. This walkway links in with other paths for cyclists, walkers and roller bladers. This network connects with local shopping areas and parks and the central area.

The waterfront is beautifully landscaped and well used throughout the year. Vancouver is making real those planning principles of a vibrant downtown with pleasant, walkable neighbourhoods. This is regenerating the city and building it for people, at a people scale. Projects such as The Residences on Georgia, by Jim Chang and Associates, The Roundhouse Community Centre by Baker McGarva Hart, the Coal House Community Centre by Henriquez and Partners are all part of this regeneration.

The Coal Harbour Community Centre was built as a public amenity, as part of the developer's contribution to the community. It is a wonderful place to be and much loved by the residents. It is built into the slope of the land, opening out onto the waterfront walkway with lots of glass. Its roof is an attractive public garden and playground. This is symbolic of the new thinking in Vancouver where good community design is central to the city's plans.

Transport is vital to the success of this regeneration and Vancouver has been developing some exciting answers to questions about population growth and increased movement. Vancouver has a basic bus and Sea Bus system that serve the city well. The Sea Buses link the downtown area with North Vancouver across the harbour; a vital linkage. A particular delight are the mini ferries that serve Granville Island. They are a unique system that is fun and commercially self-sufficient. A visit to Vancouver would not be complete without a ride on these mini ferries and a trip to Granville Island, a mixed-use area of shops, restaurants and events.

One of the outputs from Expo '86 was the SkyTrain line; this is being continued under the name of the Millennium line. It is an elevated LRT system which joins two key points on the existing line. The new section has 11 passenger stations, each reflecting local characteristics whilst being designed around the same basic concept. The line looks good and is of great value in moving people around the city in a sustainable way.

Vancouver has turned theoretical principles of sustainable city living into reality. In the process the city has addressed the issues of a growing population and their transport needs. Their solution concentrates growth in an attractive and liveable downtown that can support excellent services and transport links because of its density. These new neighbourhoods make a big contribution to a city that is increasingly attractive to live in and one that is to be enjoyed by all.

Public Realm, Glasgow

Scotland

Glasgow's Public Realm project is special because it is based on a holistic strategy that joins up a sequence of spaces. Its design is simple, but effective. It is also innovative, utilising blue lighting and all-glass covered public spaces for the first time in the United Kingdom.

Glasgow has a great tradition of art, design and architecture. It can boast many famous artists and designers, not least Charles Rennie MacIntosh. Having an industrial heritage centred on the River Clyde has meant that the large institutions of the day erected magnificent buildings, which abound in the city centre to this day.

One of the outstanding features of the modern city, however, is its transformation of the public realm, which sets off the historical and modern buildings. In 1984, *The Potential for Glasgow City Centre* was published by the Scottish Development Agency. It stressed that a healthy economy was inextricably linked to a high quality environment and that to attract new commercial headquarters, tourism and local services to the city, a major improvement of the centre was needed.

A partnership of city organisations commissioned urban designers Gillespies to

Opposite *Glasgow has an industrial heritage centred on the River Clyde*

Right The cathedral precinct project incorporated standards of design, specification and implementation, which represented a significant improvement in the environmental quality of the area

Opposite The entrance to the underground is constructed wholly in structural glass

Above The quality of Glasgow's public realm has won many accolades; people like it
Opposite The quality of design and materials, and the joining of a sequence of spaces,
make Glasgow city centre an enjoyable place to be

prepare a strategy in the early 1990s. The study emphasised that quality of life is a key factor for a successful city centre, together with the importance of environmental issues and the rising expectations of visitors. It identified initiatives to make the streets and spaces of the city more memorable and to link the institutions and cultural facilities in a network of enjoyable people places. A number of 'Milestone Projects' were identified as focal points in a network of places.

From its earliest origins until the early 18th century, Glasgow was a slow growing settlement developing along a spine from the cathedral to the River Clyde; a characteristic pattern of a medieval Scottish burgh. By the latter half of the 18th century, Glasgow's merchant classes had prospered to the extent that a new town extension was proposed, intended to house the wealthy. Between 1753 and 1796, seven new streets were laid out to the west of the existing settlement on a unique, offset grid. By 1800, St Andrews Square and St Enoch Square had also been laid out, creating the pattern for

typical Glasgow squares – a central, iconic building surrounded on three sides by terraced buildings. The architect, James Craig, constructed a second western extension to this new 'Merchant City' at the same time. This was also set out in a gridiron pattern, but in a regular grid of consistently sized blocks built on unoccupied land.

As a consequence of these grids, views within the city are long and axial. There is considerable scope for drama; for example, the view to St George's Tron. The oldest parts of the city centre show the most variations in the proportion of the streets. These characteristics are fundamental to the sense of place and urban design of Glasgow. Any interventions such as repaving, tree planting and kerb realignment had to be dealt with in a sensitive way so that they did not prejudice these unique qualities.

Glasgow was also fortunate in having a fairly extensive network of pedestrianised streets at the heart of the city, represented by three commercial streets – Buchanan Street, Sauchiehall Street and

The redesign of Buchanan Street incorporates the use of blue lighting

Argyle Street. The quality of these streets was poor and the 'Great Street Project' addressed this issue. The project included street surfaces and street furniture as well as wider issues such as the distribution of land uses, activity in the street and the long-term management and maintenance – all to encourage greater public life in the city.

The public space programme of the 1990s built on a series of milestone projects from the 1980s. The Cathedral Precinct project incorporated standards of design, specification and implementation, which represented a significant improvement in the environmental quality around the area fronting the 13th century cathedral and set a standard for other projects to follow.

Princes Square was a conversion of historic listed buildings into a glazed courtyard shopping centre and is one of the most significant landmarks from the 1980s. The incorporation of art and craftworks ensured that the development remains distinctive and a popular gathering space. Ingram Square is another project, comprising refurbished warehouses and new buildings incorporating a wide range of uses from shops and offices to residential apartments.

The Italian Centre, built on the remains of 18th century warehouses, incorporates a mix of uses and notably some of Europe's premier fashion retailers. Its integration of lively open spaces in the form of an internal courtyard and the adjacent pedestrianised John Street,

help make it one of Glasgow's finest examples of urban regeneration.

A final example of the critical role of public spaces in the regeneration of the city centre is Royal Exchange Square. This involved the remodelling of the existing space to create a high quality pedestrian environment around a new public gallery. The project reduced traffic to the absolute minimum. A raised area formed by a double step around the Gallery established a setting for the building and provides essential informal seating for people. The design is simple but enjoyable, a fine example of reclaimed space in the city centre, to provide places for people which allow the environment and the economy to prosper too.

The redesign of Buchanan Street incorporates innovative ideas including the use of blue lighting and public spaces (the entrance to the underground) constructed wholly in structural glass.

This entire process was supported by a set of guidelines and a management and maintenance regime. The guidelines cover pavements, carriageways, kerbs, street furniture and signs, soft landscaping, lighting, water, the visual arts and climate. The regeneration of Glasgow's public realm has won many accolades; people like it. The quality of design and materials and the joining of sequence of spaces make Glasgow city centre an enjoyable place to be; it is a city centre that works.

Post Office Park, Boston

USA

Many of the projects from around the world that make cities work are on a grand scale; unattainable for many smaller or less wealthy cities. The Post Office Park in Boston shows that even the transformation of small spaces can have a major impact in terms of presence and vision.

The 'pocket park' movement shows that the transformation of small-scale spaces can have a major impact. Pocket parks can improve the environment and quality of life of a city in ways that are within the reach of most cities.

New York is renowned for developing the pocket park concept, but it is to a remarkable project in Boston that we turn for our example. Post Office Square, in the heart of the financial district, is an extraordinary story of dedication and vision. An ugly, four-storey, concrete car park was transformed into a jewel of an urban space.

In 1981, a local businessman, Norman Leventhal, decided that the car park had to go. He approached the Mayor of the city and won his support. At that point he did not own the site, there was no money to turn the vision into reality and no plan. Over the next 11 years, however, the Friends of Post Office Square (FOPOS), formed as a private civic corporation comprising powerful businesses surrounding the square,

An above ground multi-storey car park was demolished and new 7-storey park was built underground
The park gives a feeling of openness and yet there are secluded places within

Opposite *An ugly, four storey car park was transformed into a jewel of an urban space*
Pavilions are glass-walled with shining copper roofs; designed to be inviting and transparent

bought the car park. The above ground multi-storey car park was demolished and a new seven-storey car park was built underground comprising 1,400 spaces with the park on the top.

Financing was totally private and complex. Initial funding for the project was raised in 1982 by the surrounding businesses to carry out the feasibility studies. Shares were then sold in FOPOS with a guarantee of a car parking space at commercial rates in the car park. The car park lease was then bought from its owners, under threat of compulsory purchase by the city. The total cost of the project was around $75 million. The square was an immediate success, its cafés, fountains, trees, grass and distinctive planting attracting many people. It is open to the public and maintained to a high standard at no cost to the city.

Initial designs were carried out at MIT by Professor Bill Porter and a management company undertook the programming. The team visited over 100 parks around the USA and prepared a guidelines book, which compared the parks at a consistent scale. The resulting programme was critical to the success of the park. It called for a 50/50 ratio of hard and soft landscape, a passive park with no children's playground, a water feature that would look good for six months of the year when it would have to be switched off, and a park that was lively and well used, subtly designed and built to a human scale.

The resulting design is conservative yet appropriate. It looks as though it belongs and has existed for some time; always a good design test. It achieves this through a clever blend of various design forms, appropriate materials, predominantly red brick and granite,

the design of the trellis and attention to planting design. The park gives a feeling of openness and yet there are secluded places within it. There are plenty of places to sit: granite walls, metal seats on walls, timber benches and moveable chairs around the cafés. Seats are so important to city spaces; they encourage people to linger and watch the world go by. They allow people to rest, so they stay longer, enjoy the city and spend more money. The central lawn is carefully sited to avoid shadows; it is the sunniest spot on the site.

The pavilions are glass-walled with shining copper roofs. They are inviting and transparent. One pavilion is the entrance to the car park, but it is more like a hotel lobby, demonstrating that even car parks can be well designed.

Art is an important element as well. A competition was held to select three artists for the artwork. The three chosen produced the trellis, the iron railings at the edges of the car park ramps and the water features. The water features are a highlight of the park. One is a glass-topped bronze urn with water tipping over the brim; the other is a temple of granite and bronze columns topped with curved glass lintels, which uses water jets to create interest.

The Post Office Park shows what can be done when the public and private sectors work together and each does what it is good at. The park shows that you don't need grand projects or large areas to create quality public spaces people can enjoy. It is a wonderful example of dedication to a vision and is an inspiration to us all. Above all it shows that cities of any size can produce areas of enjoyment that will transform their city centre and act as a catalyst for other areas.

Getting Around the City

Encouraging alternative forms of transport is a key priority for most cities

Getting Around the City

Most of the world's great cities started life long before the motorcar. However, it is the car that now dominates life in those cities and potentially presents the greatest challenge.

People move to cities because they believe their lives will be better and richer. Once there, they want to find work, be entertained, have the convenience of shops and services and ultimately the company of people. But all this requires moving around in a finite, often congested space.

Unfortunately, many of us want to make journeys at the same time and any transport system must be a series of trade-offs and compromises. There is only a finite amount of space in which to accommodate all our individual needs.

From looking across the globe a few overriding themes emerge.

One is that road space is definitely not 'free'. It is a scarce and expensive resource; possibly the scarcest resource of all given the demand. Ways have to be found to encourage people to use it in the most effective way possible.

This, however, leads to a direct assault on what most of us regard as the fundamental human right: being able to walk or drive exactly where we want and when we want – at no direct cost.

The other great reality is that the better public transport is – better in the sense of being frequent, fast and safe – then the more people will choose to use it, rather than their own cars.

The cities of Europe and the older parts of Asia have seen their centres assaulted by the car, and although many have struggled, they have still retained a sense of history and culture.

The newer cities of North America and parts of Asia, which were designed with the car in mind, have to face the challenge of creating some sense of attractive urban environment within a maze of freeways and parking lots.

The best transport projects are based around the principle of finding ways to move the maximum number of people and volume of goods. It should not be about moving vehicles. The balance between the car and cities for people has to be changed for a city to thrive.

Edinburgh's Greenways

Scotland

The Greenways in Edinburgh are a low-cost solution to improving bus transport through the reallocation of road space. It has proved very successful and offers a method that could be used by cities with limited budgets.

In 1998, as part of the City of Edinburgh's transport plan, the council introduced a novel method of giving priority to buses through reallocating the existing and limited road space available on the main radial routes into the city. The initiative is called Greenways, taking its name from the bright green colour that has been used to designate the bus lanes.

Only buses, cycles and taxis can travel in the green lanes during peak periods, giving faster and more reliable services on the routes. The system is supported by traffic signals, which sense the buses approaching and change the lights. The bus shelters are colour-coded in green to add consistency to the scheme.

The bus companies have responded positively by improving the quality of

the buses; the introduction of new, low-emission vehicles and the council-owned bus company, Lothian Buses, has designed and implemented excellent timetable and fares schedules at each bus stop. The result has been a

Above *Only buses, cycles and taxis can travel in the green lanes during peak periods*
Opposite *Edinburgh Greenways are a low-cost solution to improving bus transport through the re-allocation of road space*

The Greenways have helped turn a 30-year decline in bus passengers into a growing market. In terms of road space, 50% is given to people in cars and 50% to people in the buses

very successful project, which has helped turn a 30-year decline in bus passengers into a growing market.

There are several interesting aspects to this relatively low-cost solution to aid moving around the city. The first of these is the enforcement of the system. Red lines painted along the side of the road, as piloted in London, ensure the uninterrupted flow of the buses. Any illegal parking is addressed by issuing parking tickets or the removal of the vehicle. The red line legislation is much more strict than the normal yellow lines as there is no waiting time allowed at critical times and places. The council is also introducing cameras on the buses to target vehicles that use the Greenways illegally. The enforcement of the system has been key to its success.

Secondly, the green surface has proved a powerful enforcement tool. A special material was developed by Heriot-Watt University, a local university, to minimise the cost and ensure maximum colour retention. Experience has shown that the use of a green surface has meant that drivers feel exposed if they enter the lanes illegally. This has certainly given Greenways a high profile and strengthened the effectiveness of the enforcement of the system.

The underlying theory behind Greenways is on moving people rather than vehicles. The council realised that the city did not have the road space to allow unlimited car access with an average occupancy of just over one person. They took the view that in order to maximise the productivity of the roads they needed to get as many people and goods along them as possible, not vehicles. This meant getting more people to use public transport. In the longer term the city is planning a new tram system, but in the short term it had to be bus-based.

In Edinburgh around 20,000 people travel to work in the city centre by bus every morning and 20,000 by car. The people travelling by bus used 800 vehicles; the people travelling by car used 18,000 vehicles. In terms of efficient use of road space there was no competition. The problem was how to give buses an advantage so a switch would occur, and how to do it quickly with a small budget.

The council decided that by concentrating on moving people it was equitable to give 50% of the road space to the people in the buses and 50% to people in cars. Although some may not like the argument, it is hard to fault the thinking behind it; it is an equitable and effective policy. The council, therefore, developed a project along three major radials in the west of the city and one in the north-east. Greenways have now been in place for a number of years and have proved very successful. The initiative has won general support from the public and business, although there have been some inevitable difficulties in practice.

One of the major difficulties faced by the council was to cater for the needs of business, especially the small ones, along the routes. Edinburgh, like most European cities, has a radial road system emanating from the centre and passing through old villages, which have, over time, been subsumed into the city. The traders along these routes were concerned at loss of business, due to reduced parking and problems with delivery of goods. The council worked hard to resolve these issues by providing parking where possible, either on the route or nearby, and loading bays that could be used at certain times. Many of these problems were overcome and the council is still working with local businesses on an on-going basis.

There is no doubt that Greenways provide an innovative solution based on a system that is affordable for many cities throughout the world. It is bus-based and relatively easy to introduce. It certainly made moving around the city a whole lot easier and has played a major part in turning a situation where the number of bus passengers was declining into a growth market, for the first time in 30 years.

Bristol, The Legible City

England

Bristol is leading in many areas of urban development, but one of the most exciting is its Legible City project. Through an integrated programme of transportation, information and identity projects the Legible City aims to improve people's understanding, experience and enjoyment of the city. The concept is simple – the right message at the right time.

Whether it's a tourist trying to find a hotel, someone with a business appointment, a film goer on their way to the cinema, a cyclist going to the shops, an occasional ferry user or a parent whose child needs a toilet in a hurry – Bristol Legible City takes into account the needs of the user at every step.

One of the most influential people to impact on Bristol's thinking was Kevin Lynch (1918-1984), whose writings provided the analytical tools for

the initial development of the Legible City. He described legibility of the cityscape as '...the ease with which its parts can be organised into a coherent pattern...'. He likened the clearly marked pathways and landmarks to the symbols on a printed page. Elsewhere legibility has been described as the 'characteristic of an environment that looks as if one could explore extensively without getting lost'.

Signage and information are crucial for visitors and residents

Queen Square

THE GROVE

Arnolfini Gallery

Youth Hostel

FARR'S LANE

QUEEN SQUARE

MIDDLE AVENUE

PRINCE STREET

Jurys Bristol Hotel

NARROW QUAY

ASSEMBLY ROOMS LA

Pero's Bridge

Amphitheatre

Lloyds TSB

Information point

Four minutes

ANCHOR SQUARE

CANONS ROAD

P

P

New World Square

Wildscreen

CAMON'S ROAD

Explore

NORTH SOUTH LINK ROAD

HARBOUR WAY

Watershed Media Centre

BROAD QUAY

P

CAMONS ROAD

Swallow Royal Hotel

ANCHOR PLACE

BROAD QUAY

Bristol Cathedral

ANCHOR ROAD

TAXI

Central Promenade

ST. AUGUSTINE'S PARADE

COLLEGE GREEN

Lord Mayor's Chapel

Central Library

LOWER LAMB STREET

LWR COLLEGE ST

Hippodrome Theatre

Harvey's Wine Museum

WEST ST

College Green

DEANERY ROAD

PARTITION ST

PARK STREET

COLLEGE STREET

GAUNT'S LANE

DENMARK STREET

BRANDON STREET

PIPE LANE

UNITY STREET

You are here

P

YORK PLACE

The Council House

ST GEORGE'S ROAD

QUEEN'S PARADE

Brunel House

TRENCHARD STREET

GREAT GEORGE STREET

CULVER STREET

Bristol Ice Rink

Brandon Hill

Bristol is the major economic and cultural centre of the south west of England. However, in common with other major cities, past development has resulted in the gradual erosion and fragmentation of the traditional neighbourhoods – producing poor pedestrian orientation. In particular, research among business leaders identified a major difficulty navigating the city – with 39% describing the pedestrian signs as poor/very poor. This was seen to undermine the city's future development as a leading British and European business and cultural centre.

The Legible City is important because it recognised that
· signage and information are crucial for residents and visitors;
· street furniture has a considerable effect on the urban landscape and can help provide a sense of identity and cohesion between diverse neighbourhoods;
· good information provision can contribute towards increasing the use of public transport.

This theoretical basis has been transformed in Bristol to over 40 projects, which comprise stage one of development. These projects aim to link diverse parts of the city with consistent information, provide a clear identity and promote greater use of public transport. They include a new pedestrian signage system that constitutes a major aspect of the initial phase of the programme with a special Bristol Transit font for all the signage components. Clean looking and highly contemporary in style, its words and icons are kept to a minimum to assist all, particularly the visually impaired. The blade and monolith panels employ an innovatory 'heads-up' 3-D mapping technique.

A range of on-street I+ digital touch-screen information kiosks has been installed, providing information about tourism, leisure, accommodation, Bristol City Council and transport. Users can also send e-mails and print out maps and journey planners.

Though signs are crucial, people contact is critical, not just in obtaining information, but also in learning about the city. Navigators are a team of on-street guides providing information about the city, attractions, hotels and transport.

Opposite *Information panels employ an innovatory 'heads-up' 3-D mapping technique*
I+ digital touch-screen information kiosks are located around the city

There are four themes underlying the programme:
- place identity and way-finding
- choice of transport
- exploration
- the city by night.

Firstly, place identity and way-finding. The information to allow people to move about freely and in a relaxed manner is given both formally and informally using signs, guides, maps and landmarks around the city. Improving the choice of transport is helped by better information provision and the use of art to make the journey more attractive and enjoyable.

Exploration allows people to wander and experience areas of the city they may not discover on their own. Bristol's quaysides, for example, can offer a pleasant alternative to the main routes. Art is used to enhance these areas and encourage more people to use them. The city at night helps to promote the night-time economy, an important part of city life. Much of the daytime distinctiveness is lost in the dark and so art projects use light to animate public spaces, create new landmarks and enhance safety and confidence.

Important consideration has been given to aiding informal navigation. Those landmarks we all use to get around a city – roundabouts, petrol stations, pubs and works of art. As part of this the Legible City includes an arts programme as well as an aid to navigation. Unlike a lot of civic art this programme is an integral part of the initiative and the artists are involved in the whole process.

No city council could support such a major development alone and partnership has been a key aspect of the project. A range of public/private sector organisations worked effectively together to deliver the vision. The key factors to this successful partnership were a shared vision, a commitment to long-term solutions and long-term problems, a framework of creativity and a willingness to work together as a team.

Bristol is continuing to build on this first stage and the next phase will extend the current activity, geographically, organisationally and through integrated transport. The city was awarded £10.55 million by the UK government to extend the Legible City project into many areas of transport information and infrastructure, including new shelters for the proposed tram system and a programme of showcase bus routes. Bristol is determined to maintain the city as the most legible in the UK, and perhaps Europe.

Good information provision can contribute towards the use of public transport

Smart card technology gives users easy access to the whole network of bikes
A roving dispatch vehicle ensures an even supply of bikes in the docking stations

Cycling in Rennes and Groningen

France and the Netherlands

Cities around the world today are facing major problems with the build-up of traffic and congestion. In order to reverse the damage being caused to the environment, city authorities are urging the public to reduce private car use by introducing restrictions in city centres, promoting public transport and encouraging alternative forms of travel, in particular cycling.

The city of Rennes in France created a pedestrianised centre to the city, but still suffered from serious traffic congestion and pollution. To address this problem a cycle scheme was considered to be one of the most appropriate ways to enable convenient and environmentally friendly transport to its main shopping and historical areas.

In June 1998, the city of Rennes launched an innovative bicycle loan scheme called SmartBike. The system is funded entirely by advertising revenue from the city's street furniture contract and consists of 25 docking stations located throughout the city, 200 bikes and 2,000 smart cards for user operation. Users only need to pay a deposit for access to a smart card.

A docking station was installed in each of 12 'neighbourhoods', with a further 13 stations positioned next to 'cyclists generating points', such as university grounds,

SmartBike is very popular among the city students

The system is funded entirely by advertising revenue
Over 60% of trips in Groningen are made on bicycles
Dedicated and safe cycle lanes make cycling more popular

train stations, main bus interchange terminals, shopping centres and major administrative buildings, and on park-and-ride locations.

The smart card issued to users incorporates a personalised microchip that gives them easy access to the whole network of bikes in the city. It also records who has possession of a bike at any given time and tracks its location. This provides the city with all relevant security information, including the user's identity and when a bike is returned.

The smart cards were split into three areas of allocation with 1,320 being distributed among Rennes city residents, 280 allocated to the residents of the district of Rennes – which covers 32 neighbouring towns and villages, and a further 400 reserved for students of Rennes universities.

The smart cards were distributed free of charge, on a first-come, first-served basis. In return, the user was required to sign a contract which presented the terms and conditions of using the system. These included a waiver of all liability in the event of a breakdown or theft, as long as the user complied with a few simple rules and could guarantee personal insurance cover in case of any accidents. Also, in order to join the scheme, each applicant had to provide two forms of identification.

Only one smart card was issued per household, allowing the user to loan a bike for a maximum time of two hours, with further loans permitted throughout the day, for two-hour periods at a time.

On-line monitoring protects the bikes from theft and vandalism and locates them anywhere in the network. It also communicates with a roving dispatch vehicle, whose crew ensure an even supply of bikes in the stations. In addition, they carry out regular maintenance and routine cleaning and remove any damaged or non-functional bikes to be repaired in a local centre.

In 1999, over 40,000 trips using SmartBike were recorded and typically the average journey lasted 26 minutes. In more than two thirds of cases, the bike was returned to a different station from where it was borrowed. The number of loans was found to have increased steadily over the year, with lower levels of rental during the peak holiday periods and over weekends. Usage was spread throughout the day, with a significant increase during peak commuting hours.

These results highlighted the success of the system by proving that a great many people were using the bikes to get to and from their place of work or study – a finding supported by the fact that more than 50% of bikes loaned were situated next to universities, at a bus interchange point or following a park-and-ride pattern.

The SmartBike system in Rennes is considered to have been highly successful and has become a case study for other cities around the world. Cycling is growing in popularity and many cities are now pursing cycling-friendly policies to reduce traffic congestion and make city centres a more pleasant environment to live and work.

The city of Groningen in the Netherlands is another good example of cycling. The council took the bold step of banning the car from one square kilometre of the old town and in doing this made a conscious decision to promote cycling. They also backed their aspirations with financial support. This enabled the initiation of schemes such as guarded cycle parks and the creation of safe, dedicated cycle routes throughout the city.

The success of this strategy has been particularly impressive. Over 60% of all trips in Groningen are now made on bicycles and the city was voted the third best city in the world for cycling, after two Chinese cities. The key was that the council addressed the two biggest problems for those who aspired to cycle in cities: safe and pleasant routes and secure parking.

In an age where many cities around the world are struggling to increase the use of cycling, the cities of Groningen and Rennes stand out as beacons of hope.

Bus shelters have automatic doors that align with the bus and allow mass boarding

Curitiba

Brazil

Curitiba in Brazil has shown that large numbers of people can be efficiently moved around a city by bus without investing huge sums of money. By establishing a growth plan for the city and building a public transport system around it, Curitiba has created a model for the rest of the world.

Curitiba is one of the fastest growing cities in Brazil with a population of 1.6 million inhabitants. Being the capital of the State of Parana, it is also the administrative and political centre. Rapid economic and demographic growth in the last few decades have made the city an important transport hub and a commercial centre for agricultural goods.

The main characteristic of Curitiba, however, is the innovative way its urban problems were resolved, especially the planning and transport systems. During the rapid expansion of Brazil in the 1960s, Curitiba chose a planning

framework that integrated all elements of the urban system. While most Brazilian cities were planning for cars, Curitiba was far-sighted enough to plan for an excellent and novel public transport system that linked with land-use planning. The key concept

Above *Large numbers of people can be moved efficiently by bus without investing huge sums of money*
Opposite *Express buses run along a segregated central lane*

was to encourage Curitiba's expansion along linear corridors centred on express bus ways. Traditional city centre areas were preserved and designed to accommodate cultural heritage, employment and people-orientated policies.

The public transport system is designed around five main axes each based on a 'Trinary' road system, with each axis having a segregated central lane for express buses. These express lanes enable a considerably higher average bus speed without jeopardising passenger safety. There are around 58 exclusive lanes that criss-cross the city along its north, south, east, west and southwest axes. The axes

are complemented by 270 km of feeder routes and 185km of interdistrict routes, serving about 65% of the urban area. When added to the conventional bus system, Curitiba's transportation system covers the entire municipal area.

A key aspect of the system is the combination of low operational costs and high quality service. Around 1.9 million passengers are transported daily with 89% user satisfaction rating. It also has an integrated tariff, which allows people to travel throughout the city on one ticket. Those commuting long distances, mainly low-income families, are subsidised by those making shorter trips. Within the

integrated network are over 1,900 buses, making 14,000 journeys daily, totalling 316,000km every day.

Although Curitiba has more cars per capita than any other Brazilian city, it does not suffer problems, due to the inexpensive way it can move large numbers of people around effectively and efficiently. Around 28% of passengers previously travelled by car so the system helps improve air quality as well as reducing congestion and fuel consumption. The city has low levels of air pollution.

The ticketing system is fully automatic and specially designed bus shelters are equipped with barrier and off-ticketing machines. The shelters are well designed and innovative. Some are particularly unique in that they allow rapid mass boarding of the buses as ticketing has been carried out beforehand and the shelter's automatic doors are aligned with the bus doors.

Developing alongside the transport system is a complementary planning system. The creation of the Curitiba Research and Urban Planning Institute (IPPUC) led the revolution in thinking; it was a laboratory of ideas that changed the face of the city and prepared it for the future. The IPPUC played a major role in the process of defining the plan to accommodate Curitiba's projected growth. By establishing orderly development along and around the express transportation routes, the master plan enabled the population to see the global picture, as well as their own 'Curitibano'. This focused approach to urban planning and transportation has enabled Curitiba to improve the environmental and cultural aspects of the city centre.

Many old buildings have been preserved and many areas pedestrianised, like the famous Flowers Street in the downtown district, which was the first pedestrian street in the country. Flowers Street is now a well-used meeting and leisure place. These improvements attract more people to the city centre and enhance the economy. Curitiba also created the first 24-hour street, an open space with dozens of shops catering for a range of needs. This includes bars, chemists, laundry, flower shops and mini-markets. All of this creation of life and vibrancy in the city stems from a first class way of moving around and a planned approach to the development of the city in harmony with the transport system.

Curitiba has now one of the highest averages of green space per inhabitant in South America due to its commitment to preserve woods and parks. During the weekend a free bus service operates on the pro-park line. It utilises older buses to carry people from the downtown area to the city's numerous parks.

Curitiba demonstrates that you can move people by bus in an acceptable and efficient way around a growing city if you follow certain principles. A growth plan for the city was established and the transport system was built around the development areas and along a series of corridors. The city succeeded in using a low technology bus system and joined local community plans and involvement with the global plans for the city. Last, but not least, the initiative showed the importance of civic leadership through Major Jaime Lerner, who was the inspiration behind it all.

Curitiba is a fascinating place where you can move freely, whether in the city centre or through its network of parks. Curitiba has won many prizes for its pioneering work over the last 30 years. It is a city that works!

Landscape architects were used to ensure consistency of design with the cityscape

The Strasbourg LRT

France

A growing demand for cars and the problems they bring gave impetus to the city's leaders to improve public transport. This led to the implementation of an LRT in 1997, a system that has demonstrated it is possible to create a positive image of public transport and ultimately get people out of their cars.

One of the best ways to move about a city is by tram, or as it is called nowadays, Light Rapid Transit (LRT). An LRT can become a symbol for a city that speaks of vitality, efficiency and beauty. There is something romantic and exciting about the modern tram that touches distant memories of our childhood and propels us into the 21st century at the same time.

There is no doubt that one of the best examples of all these aspects is the Strasbourg LRT. It is efficient, it is effective, but most of all it is beautiful. It is a joy to see and has improved the image and efficiency of Strasbourg. It is

a powerful example of how a transport system can become a symbol that helps mould the image of a city.

The basis of the LRT was a decision by Strasbourg Conurbation to define an integrated urban development strategy that would be less space consuming while ensuring

Bus and tram interchanges improve efficiency and allow customers to use the same ticket for both modes of transport

The LRT moves people in comfort and style

*The system has become a symbol for the city that speaks of vitality,
efficiency and beauty*

maximum mobility of people and goods. It would also be a strategy that would support the economic development of the city and its conurbation. Transport was a central part of the strategy. The application of the transport policy aims to establish a coherent and long-term harmonious coexistence between the various means of transport, whilst addressing social unity and quality of life.

According to a city survey conducted in 1988, 74% of commuting was done by car and 11% by public transport. Furthermore, car traffic was growing. It was recognised that the city could not cope with this growing demand for car traffic and all the problems it brought. This gave impetus to the city's leaders to improve public transport.

In 1997, three years after commissioning the LRT, public transport usage had increased by 43%. The under-35 age group has responded particularly well, a group normally very car orientated. Pedestrian activity and cycling had also increased in residential areas adjacent to the LRT. If it is done well, people will use public transport.

The fixed nature of the LRT line gives confidence to developers and has been responsible for increasing rents and property values around the transit lines. There are also significant economic advantages in providing an LRT.

To strengthen image, much care and attention was given to the design of the line as well as the vehicle. Landscape architects were used to design the covering of the stations, the treatment applied to the road and footways, the trees, the street lighting and LRT infrastructure, to ensure consistency with the cityscape. The identity of each area crossed by the LRT was highlighted by accentuating the beauty of the area, giving a face-lift to frontages or even carrying out refurbishment works.

The tram, which has been designed as the backbone of the transport system, is helpful in reorganising commuting patterns and enhancing the rest of the public transport system through integration and creating new culture. The LRT also gives opportunities to redesign areas of public space.

Due to its innovative and non-polluting nature, the LRT offers passengers increased comfort, improved service and an enjoyable experience. The 22 stations along the 12km of the A and D lines serve over 100,000 inhabitants. Every day, about 77,000 people use the LRT. This number doubled at the end of 2000 when the 24 stations of the B and C lines became operational.

The completion of the four lines created a network that also facilitated the expansion of the bus network to include regional routes. Today, the LRT is used by 65% of city workers, a remarkable turn-around in a relatively short period. The longer-term vision is to have a 35km network of lines by 2010, which will link up to the major road and rail networks at strategic points. The system will be totally integrated at this time.

The first tramline cost 296 million Euros and the second a further 248 million Euros. Ownership, management and development are entrusted to the CTS, a jointly funded company in charge of the public transport network in the city. In 1999, with LRT line A in operation, CTS earned 7 Euro/km against an operational cost of 5 Euro/km.

The system is supported by a number of other measures, which include inter-modal marketing initiatives. For example, fixed-cost day-tickets are available for car drivers using the park-and-ride facilities, cycles can be carried on-board at no additional cost outside peak periods and job seekers pay a lower fare. Customers can also use the same ticket on the LRT and the bus. In the evening, a collective taxi service is available at some of the bus and LRT stations to take people to the bus stop closest to their homes.

The Strasbourg LRT demonstrates that it is possible to get people out of their cars as well as improving the environment, the economy and quality of life. They need not be in conflict. It is possible to design a transport system that is beautiful as well as functional; a system that generates a positive image. The Strasbourg LRT is a great example of efficiently moving people around a city in comfort and style. Strasbourg has shown it can be done.

The Portland Streetcar, Oregon

USA

The City of Portland has resurrected the streetcar, not for nostalgia, but as a means to strengthen the city centre's close-in neighbourhoods and link them with nearby commercial, institutional, cultural and recreational activities. The project has provided a catalyst for new downtown development and complements the regional rail service.

Portland has long been acknowledged as one of America's most liveable cities. It is a city that has led by example in terms of addressing transportation and land use in a coordinated and complementary fashion. The impressive Tri-Met Metropolitan Area Express (MAX) light rail system has been a product of this process and a solution for regional transportation. However, Portland has now gone one step further and resurrected a very localised and central transportation system in the form of the Streetcar.

The Portland Streetcar is a 3.5km line being built through downtown Portland, connecting a number of the close-in neighbourhoods. It is designed to fit into Portland's neighbourhoods, not change them.

These thriving neighbourhoods are what make Portland so liveable. They are enclaves of diverse residential, commercial and cultural activity. The city wishes to commit resources to

Opposite *The Portland Streetcar is a 3.5 km line built through downtown Portland, connecting a number of the close-in neighbourhoods*

Above In keeping with the theme of simplicity, the streetcar stops are extensions of the pathway out in the parking lane
Right The cars have 30 seats and space for 87 standing passengers

strengthen these and foster the development of new ones. Good local transportation is at the core of how successfully this occurs. Portland is seeking better to link educational centres, work destinations, shopping and entertainment areas, and old and new residences with the downtown Streetcar line.

A general principle of the project was 'This is not light rail; it's a streetcar'. The city purposefully intended to differentiate it from the scale, investment and market of the MAX. The Streetcar does however intersect with MAX, providing people with a direct connection to the airport and the wider regional area.

Planning for the Streetcar began in 1989, but the project itself was not finally completed until 2001. A non-profit corporation, Portland Streetcar Inc., which had a board made up of directors form the public and private sector and a citizens advisory committee, was responsible for implementing the project.

The $42 million project capital costs were funded in a unique manner utilising several revenue sources: those included the sale of municipal bonds backed by a 20 cent per hour increase in city-owned downtown car parks, a small federal grant and assessments from a newly designated local improvement district. The latter was

An innovative form of funding and the low-cost system make the
Streetcar an attractive and affordable way of getting around the city

applied to property owners in the vicinity of the Streetcar line and involved a number of factors intended to recognise the wide diversity of properties and land uses along the line and the direct benefit they would gain from the Streetcar. This approach was readily accepted by more than half of the property owners, who understood these benefits and voluntarily agreed to tax themselves.

The $8.3 million derived from this 'voluntary tax' was fixed to allay fears that the property owners would be subject to further assessments if the costs of the project rose above initial projections. The operating costs are about $2.5 million per year and are funded two-thirds from Tri-Met and the rest from fares, advertising and parking revenues along the line.

Obtaining the new Streetcars was a particular challenge. The MAX light rail vehicle was out of scale with the environment and overdesigned for the purpose of city centre running. The Streetcar would be operating in mixed traffic at low speeds, stopping frequently, crossing residential areas where even buses are barely welcomed, so this called for a smaller, more people-friendly vehicle.

With the need initially for only four cars and a restricted budget, a new design was not possible either. After a tendering process Inekon/Skoda, a major producer of railcars in former Eastern European countries, was chosen. The company offered an adaption of its new Astra design being built for a number of cities in the Czech Republic. The Streetcar is 20m long, 2.46m wide, double ended and double-sided. The cars have 30 seats and space for 87 standing. All cars are air-conditioned. Much attention has been paid to the appearance of the cars. Each has a unique paint scheme and has a bright and welcoming interior achieved through the combination of large windows, lighting and the patterns and colours selected for the interior fittings.

In keeping with the theme of simplicity, the Streetcar stops are extensions of the pathways out into the parking lane. The platform height varies to allow for wheelchairs and differing boarding heights for bus and Streetcars. The platforms are well designed and fitted with a modest shelter, leaning rails, transit signs and litter bins. The simple design reflects the Streetcar philosophy and minimises costs.

Traffic signal pre-emption is provided along the entire route. Where the Streetcar's movement conflicts with general traffic the Streetcar can communicate with the traffic signal and gain priority. The fare structure is integrated with the MAX light rail system. However, much of the Streetcar network is in the downtown free-fare zone – Fareless Square – so fare collection is not as intense as it could be. For this reason, and to keep costs down, there are no ticket machines at the stops. Tickets are also valid on the Tri-Met's buses.

One of the most impressive elements of the Portland Streetcar is the way it interacts and fits in with the surrounding land use. At one of the terminus stations it goes through and under an area of the university new development. Its design is simple yet elegant; it is in harmony with the feel of the neighbourhoods. The innovative form of funding and the low cost system make this an attractive and affordable way to get around the city.

The busway stations were designed to be contemporary symbols, achieving a consistent and recognisable look

The Brisbane Busway

Australia

The Brisbane Busway has shown that a quality bus system can attract people in large numbers, even from cars. It has achieved this through providing an attractive, reliable service, good integration and information and a commitment to good design down to the last detail.

In 1995, Queensland State Government, in partnership with the Commonwealth (Australian) Government and the local governments of the region, developed the Integrated Transport Plan for South East Queensland (IRTP). The IRTP was the blueprint for developing the transport system to manage the movement of people and goods. A key aspect of the strategy was focused on public transport.

In 1992, public transport's share of the travel market was 7% and was predicted to decline to 6.3% of all trips by 2011, if the trend continued. One project chosen to address this decline was a 75km network of busways to complement the heavy rail network.

The Queensland government approved the South East Transit (SET)

Project to manage the construction of over 16km of dedicated two-lane, two-way roadway for buses between Brisbane Central Business District and Eight Mile Plains. The first section of busway between the Central Business District and Woollongabba, and Eight Mile Plains, opened in April 2001.

Real-time information keeps passengers informed

*The project developed over 16km of dedicated two-lane, two-way
roadway for buses*

Land values in the suburbs with busway stations increased by over 20% in three months

The busway has been a great success, carrying an average of 60,000 passengers a day. In the first 12 months of operation an extra 1 million passengers used the core bus service; an increase of 45% compared with the previous year. Land values in certain suburbs with busway stations have increased by over 20% in three months, compared with a rise of only 6% in adjacent suburbs without direct access.

The busway stations were designed to be contemporary symbols, achieving a consistent, recognisable look irrespective of their location. The effect is visually pleasing; the design promotes a quality image, which is safe and accessible. The attention to detail is stunning; from the beautifully designed drinking fountains to the attractive landscaping. Static and electronic signing is also well designed and clear. There is no graffiti or litter, even after two years of operation. This is due to a strictly enforced management and maintenance regime that removes any litter or graffiti quickly. The busway has truly transformed the image of public transport in Brisbane and has been rewarded by passengers using it in ever increasing numbers.

The busway has also been designed to connect into other transport services. For example, the busway stations at Buranda and South Bank were built adjacent to train stations. South Bank busway station also connects with the shuttle bus service between Kangaroo Point and Morningside and is a short walk to the City Cat cross-river ferry service. Many of the busway stations connect into the local bus services and have park-and-ride and kiss-and-ride provision.

The clever use of technology on the busway has contributed towards Queensland's reputation as the Smart State. This is best seen at the busway operations centre, which coordinates an Intelligent Transport System to manage the busway. There are 140 CCTV security services, which are monitored 24-hours a day. A Voice Switching System, activated through touch-screen technology, manages the public address system, emergency telephones, lifts and tunnels and two-way radio communication with the drivers and the city council. RAPID uses detector loops in the road and transponders on the buses to track the location of buses on the busway and real-time arrival information is fed to the stations.

The Queensland government allocated $8 million for landscaping of the busway; key to the success of the project. Two objectives drove the landscape design: a quality entry to the city of Brisbane and protectiion and enhancment of the existing environment. The result is a landscaping provision of real quality that raises the image of public transport as never before in Queensland. Visually impressive, it contributes much to the pleasure of riding on the busway.

The busway is a great success and will benefit the economy and environment of Brisbane for years to come. Market research has shown that 57% of busway users have reduced their reliance on the car since the busway opened. For every full bus there are 40 less cars to add to the congestion of Brisbane. The use of low-emission natural gas buses adds to the environmental benefit. It is truly an enjoyable, cost-effective and efficient way to get around the city of Brisbane.

Singapore Road Pricing

Singapore

For almost two centuries, travel has been getting easier, cheaper and faster. But many urban transport systems in industrial countries are reaching full capacity. Economists agree that the best way to tackle the growing problem of overcrowded roads is to introduce tolls at peak times. In the field of transportation, road pricing or congestion charging has long been associated with Singapore, but now many other cities are planning to follow suit.

The big concern used to be pollution, but cleaner and more efficient engines have reduced damaging emissions from cars, and this trend looks to continue. Today, the emphasis is shifting to the physical space cars occupy on limited space; and the way roads continue to consume finite land. The public will no longer tolerate the destruction of city centres or green fields for more roads.

It has been suggested that the economic consequences of congestion are enormous. These economic costs include lost time, wasted fuel and

increased vehicle operating costs, estimated to account for between 2 and 4 per cent of Gross Domestic Product. A 1999 study by Texas A&M University found that congestion cost US drivers $72bn in 1997, or 3.7% of GDP.

Above *The smart card is inserted into an in-vehicle unit*
Opposite *Road pricing has long been associated with Singapore*

Opposite Technology has helped make the expansion of the original road-pricing scheme possible Traffic volume has dropped by about 10-15% during ERP operation hours

Until the recent introduction into London, the most ambitious urban charging scheme has been Singapore, where it was first launched in June 1975. The initial system was manual, based on paper permits and applicable during the morning peak period only. Over the past 27 years it has evolved into an electronic version that operates almost throughout the entire day.

Originally there were two manual road pricing schemes used in Singapore, namely the Area Licensing Scheme (ALS) and the Road Pricing Scheme (RPS). The ALS was in place for 23 years before being replaced by an electronic version called the Electronic Road Pricing Scheme (ERP). The RPS was implemented progressively on expressways from 1995, and subsequently also replaced by the ERP in 1998. Both schemes were based on the need for paper licences to be purchased prior to the passage through control points.

The ALS covered the more congested parts of the Central Business District, known as the Restricted Zone. To gain access to this zone, non-exempt vehicles needed to purchase and display an ALS area licence.

The scheme covered two periods, the restricted rush hour periods of 7.30am to 10.15am and 4.30pm to 7pm, and the inter-peak periods between 10.15am and 4.30pm. Saturdays had slightly different charging times and Sundays were exempt. Hence, there were two categories of licence, known as 'whole day licences' and 'part-day licences'. Only scheduled public buses and emergency vehicles were exempted.

The initial drop in traffic entering the restricted zones was 44%, but it crept up to 31% by 1988. This was despite the growth by a third in employment in the city and a 77% increase in vehicle population during the same period.

Being manual schemes, both the ALS and RPS had certain limitations. They were heavily labour intensive and human enforcement by visual means was prone to error. Manual licences also offered

Opposite *When the vehicle passes through the ERP gantry, the appropriate charge is deducted from the smart card*

vehicles unlimited entries to the restricted zone, often resulting in the illegal transfer of permits between vehicles. There was also a rush to enter restricted zones just before or after the restricted hours because of the changes in fee.

Due to the shortcomings of the manual system, the search for a more efficient technology began in the early 1990s. A comprehensive test programme of a Dedicated Short-Range Communication electronic road pricing scheme started in December 1996. Over 4.8 million vehicles were clocked before the test was considered successful.

The ERP system is designed to be simple to use. All that it requires of the user is to insert the smart card into an in-vehicle unit (IU), whereby a diagnostic check is done automatically to ensure that both the IU and smart card are in working condition. If there is a problem it will alert the user.

As a vehicle passes through the ERP gantry, the appropriate ERP charge is deducted from the smart card. When there is insufficient cash, no smart card, or IU, the enforcement cameras in the gantry take a picture of the rear of the offending vehicle and the appropriate penalties will be issued.

Traffic volume into the Central Business District (CBD) has been reduced by about 10-15% during the ERP operation hours, as compared to the original manual scheme (ALS). The major difference between the manual system and the ERP is that the latter creates a charge for each passing. The ERP has therefore influenced particularly the behaviour of those who made multiple trips into the CBD – this was estimated to be about 23%.

Road pricing in Singapore has been effective in managing congestion on roads in the CBD since its inception in 1975, and in recent years on expressways and other major roads outside the CBD. Technology has helped to make the expansion of the original road-pricing scheme possible; and the authorities are still keeping a close eye on the new developments in road pricing technology to further enhance the present ERP system.

The Singapore system has demonstrated that by addressing the latent demand for private cars to enter the city at peak times, pricing can considerably improve the ability to move about the city. Over the next few years it is foreseen that a number of other congested cities will follow suit.

The system offers immediate personal service
Journeys are predicted to be three times quicker than by bus, car or rail

The ULTra System, Cardiff

Wales

ULTra is an innovative and novel way to get about a city. It is cheap, yet provides a high level of service to the user, which falls between conventional public transport and the taxi. It is also futuristic and fun.

All of the case studies in this book have been constructed and are operating successfully. The ULTra system is still being tested and a full application is not yet operational. The concept is so novel and exciting however, that it was thought appropriate to include in the book. It is in keeping with the visionary tone of the case studies to highlight a transport system that is futuristic, novel, fun and operates at one third of the cost of light rail.

The ULTra system has been under development since 1995. The concept was developed initially by the Advanced Transport Group at the University of Bristol. Advanced Transport Systems Ltd (ATS), Arup and Amec are now

developing it. The project is supported by the National Endowment for Science and the Arts, the Department of Trade and Industry and the Department for Transport. A number of potential applications are being researched and planned.

ULTra produces zero pollution and is quiet
The average speed is about 40kph

Futuristic and fun

The ULTra is an on-demand system of driverless automatic taxis travelling on their own guideway network. It offers immediate personal service, provides journeys that are three times quicker than bus, car, light or heavy rail, costs less to operate than any other form of mechanical public transport, uses much less energy than other forms of public transport and is quiet and efficient with zero pollution.

In October 1999 ULTra was given a government grant to build a prototype vehicle. This was followed in 2000 with further support for the design, manufacture and testing of the prototype system, including provision of a test track in Cardiff.

A series of studies has been undertaken in Cardiff to demonstrate the viability and relative service level of an ULTra system, compared to the requirements of the Cardiff Bay development and city centre areas, both pilot locations chosen for these studies. These studies have shown the benefits to users and non-users of the system, local businesses and the city of Cardiff. One example of this is that the analysis in terms of fatalities, serious and slight injuries for the Cardiff area shows a reduction of about 50 accidents per annum.

The risk of failure is low because it uses existing, proven technology, one year of testing has already been completed, the test track includes all critical city application features and an extensive, maturity testing and commissioning programme will be completed before commercial operation. Detailed discussions with HM Rail Inspectorate have been held over several years. The Concept Safety Paper developed by ATS has received a letter of no objection from HMRI, who have also commended the company on their exceptionally thorough approach to safety issues.

The ULTra guideway has the same capacity as a motorway lane, yet is a tenth of the cost and uses a third of the land. The ULTra average speed is about 40 kph and journeys are non-stop because stations are off-line. More than 80% of ULTra passengers will have no waiting time; with 95% waiting less that 1 minute, even at peak times. The ULTra emits less than a tenth of the emissions of congested traffic, produces zero pollution and is quiet because of its electric drive and rubber wheels. The vehicles are fully accessible to all users including the disabled, cyclists and users with pushchairs.

The visual intrusion of the overhead guideway may be an issue for some. The designers have worked hard to reduce the depth of the structure to 45cm (18in). The majority of people surveyed regard this as acceptable.

Fare level will be comparable to a single bus user but, in the case of ULTra, this would apply for use of the vehicle. This means that couples or families will receive a significant cost benefit. It is estimated that the system will cost between a third and half of the equivalent light rail alternative.

ULTra is a novel and exciting answer to modern day traffic congestion. It is an affordable way to get around the city from both a provider and user point of view. It is also fun and offers an impressive range of advantages. Here's hoping that in the near future we can all experience the ultimate on the ULTra.

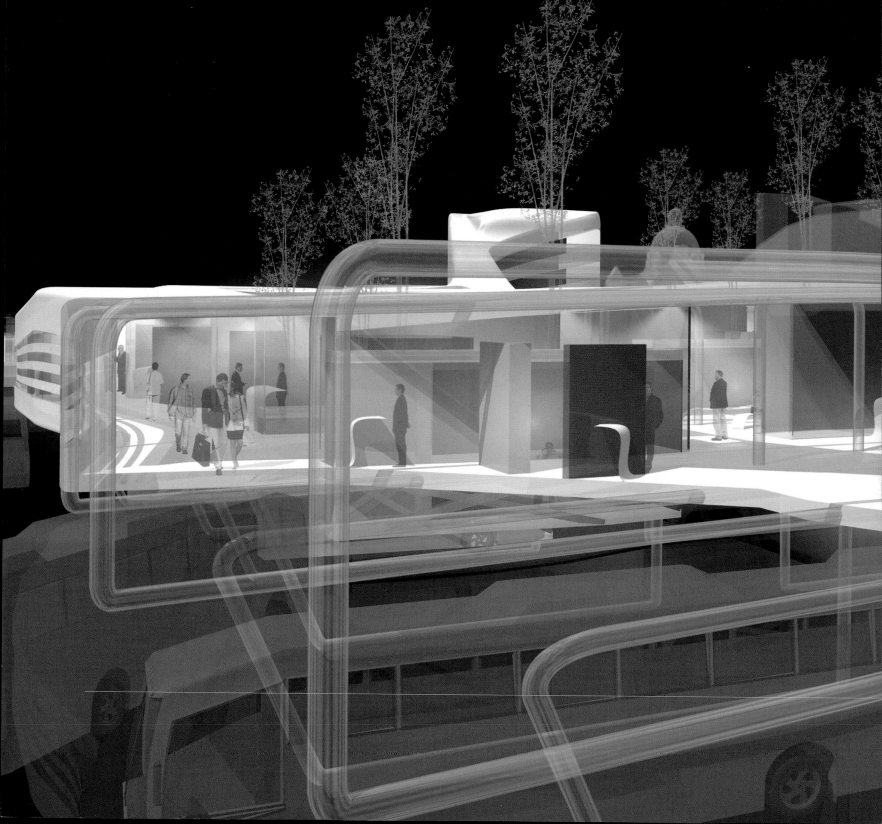

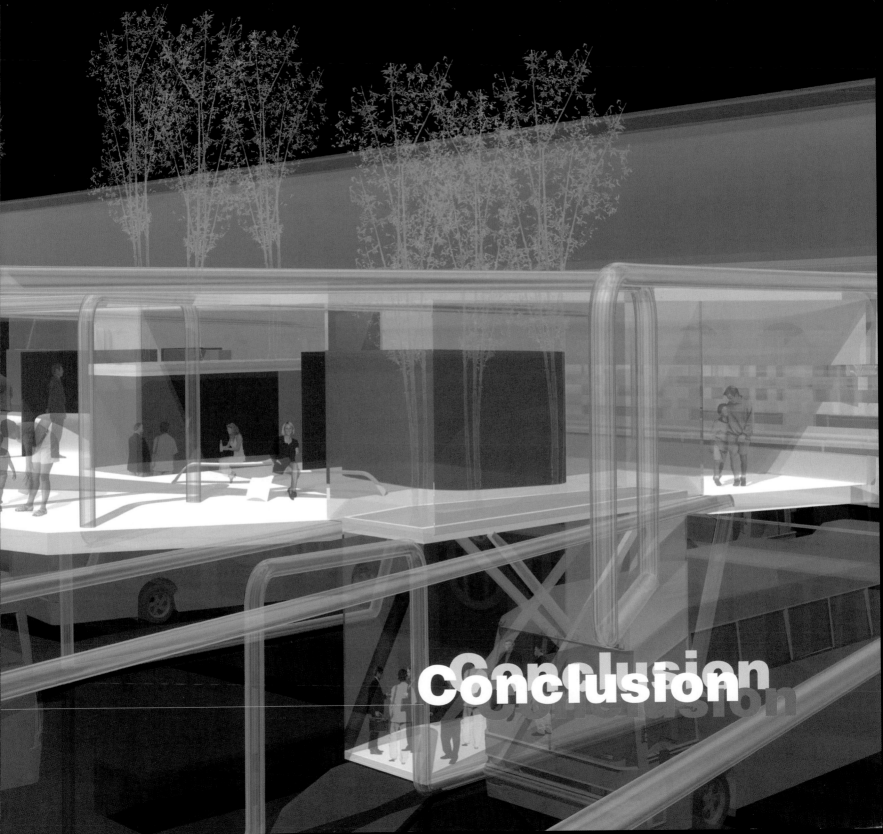

Conclusion

Conclusion

This collection of examples is just that – a collection of examples. There are very many successful ideas that do indeed 'make cities work' that have not found space in this book.

So, what lessons have we learned in looking around the world for inspiration?

The first is that cities have to find a solution to the car. Cities don't work at all unless people can get into them and move around relatively easily. If public transport systems are not adequate and if distances are too great for walking, then all of us inevitably want to use our car.

At its simplest, the reality is that road space has to be rationed in some way. It is not a free public good. The arrival of satellite technology means it is almost inevitable that major cities/states in the future will charge for the use of roads in the same way that the electricity, gas or telephone companies charge for the use of their utilities. The exact mechanism of universal road pricing is not yet clear, but the fact that we have to is.

Second is that developments, even the most spectacular, have to be on a human scale. All aspects of the city – arriving, enjoying it and getting around – are human activities. Buildings and spaces, no matter how large, must be designed with the individual in mind.

Third is that information is the key. Cities can be vast, disturbing places. People need to know how they work and which way is up. Initiatives like Bristol's Legible City are specifically aimed at this, but all the best cities spend a lot of time and effort telling us, the people, how to use them well.

Fourth, it is people, often one individual, who make things happen: city mayors with a mission, architects with a vision, businessmen with commitment and planning chiefs with a passion to get things done. Organisations formed by such urban heroes with a special objective in mind, such as the Grand Central Partnership in New York, the Friends of Post Office Park in Boston and the Asociacion de Comerciantes y Professionales in Marbella, will make things happen. By and large, government committees and teams of civil servants do not actually achieve results; they set the agenda. Planning is for government – doing is for individuals with grit, passion and vision.

Cities are a fact of life. For the vast majority of us, and our children, they will define our lives.

This book argues that it is the cumulative effect of visionary ideas, sometimes small, that make cities work. Politicians and planners need to seek out these ideas, nurture and support them and the urban heroes associated with them, and help release them to liberate our cities.

Opposite *The Millennium Line in Vancouver, an elevated LRT system*
Previous spread *Oliverio Najmias [najmias|arquitectos] + Luis Maria Etchegorry, Transport Exchange System [TES], for La Plata, Argentina, 2002.*

Urban Heroes

As we have searched the world for modern examples of excellence in arriving, enjoying and moving around cities, one thing has been evident in the majority of the success stories: the presence of a champion – an individual who has the vision, commitment and personal strength necessary to ensure successful completion of a project. Such people can best be described as modern day urban heroes.

Many of these individuals will have had to endure severe criticism from those who doubted their vision or could see all the difficulties that lay ahead. But our heroes will have continued to show commendable civic leadership in the face of such pressures. Whether from the public or private sector, they have proved that when the two come together in a partnership of trust and commitment – things begin to happen.

This element is of such importance that we have highlighted a few of our favourite urban heroes from the case studies included within this book. There are, of course, many more around the world and we acknowledge, salute them and wish them success in all that they do.

Helen Holland

Helen Holland was Cabinet Member for Environment, Transport and Leisure at Bristol City Council and latterly Deputy Leader of the Council until May 2003. She also served on a number of Community and Business Partnership boards including the South-West of England Regional Development Agency. She has shown leadership and commitment over a number of years to the transport and regeneration agenda and has introduced initiatives that have transformed the city.

One of these initiatives culminated in Bristol being awarded Centre of Excellence status by the UK government for its Transport Plan in March 2001. With this, Holland was recognised as a champion of sustainable and integrated transport. The transport strategy addressed social inclusion issues as well as restraint issues.

Another of these initiatives is the Legible City, which contains visionary concepts using the application of technology in real-time information at kiosks, and innovative signing and lighting.

She has presented numerous papers at local, European and international events and was central to the UK Government Changing Development Partnership and the Europrice network of European cities. She is also a member of the UK Commission for Integrated Transport. In 2001, at the UK National Transport Awards, she was given the accolade of Local Authority Transport Personality of the Year. Her dedication to the principles of city living and sustainable transport has made her a leader in her field.

Gordon Price

Gordon Price served on Vancouver City Council for 16 years. During that time he fought to protect historic buildings and promoted high-density residential developments in the city centre. Saving old buildings and having more people in smaller areas he believes are both sustainable policies, which support the vitality of the city.

During his 16 years on the council he helped create the system of cycle routes that now covers the central area. He organised the Clouds of Change task force, which reported on air pollution. But Price, who retired from the council towards the end of 2002, has shaped the city in a dramatic way. The West End has become a model urban neigh-

bourhood and the Concord Pacific and Downtown South neighbourhoods are emerging as significant success stories. He has been active at every stage of the 10-year downtown housing boom in Vancouver and has used it to transform the central area using ideas that range from innovative, specific concepts to building liveable communities.

Price got his inspiration from books like Jane Jacob's *Death and Life of Great American Cities* and his love of cycling enabled him to experience many communities first hand. Touring the city on his bike he analysed the city's West End block by block, studied census data and developed his vision for high-density living. Price's work then acted as a catalyst for other areas. The Coal Harbour and False Creek waterfronts emerged, incorporating community facilities and shops, which prosper because of the density of people within walking distance. One very high quality food store in the Downtown area has no parking whatsoever; it doesn't need it and is thriving.

Price is passionate about recreating sustainable, dense, liveable communities and his years at Vancouver City Council have left a remarkable legacy for the city.

Maureen Hayes

To deliver real improvements for the community requires a combination of courage, leadership, perceptiveness and persistence. Maureen Hayes, in her capacity as Chairperson of Transport and Traffic on Brisbane City Council, one of the largest councils in the world, has shown just such rare and special attributes.

Two of the most tangible results of her vision are the Citycat ferry service on the Brisbane River and the South-East Transit Busway, a $0.5 billion transit solution, both of which have delivered record public transport patronage growth for the city.

Hayes, who has been in her role for over a decade, has overseen the creation of these world-class solutions from inception to service delivery. The origin of the Brisbane busway lay in her visit to Ottawa (the home of the first such infrastructure) in the very early days after her election. She immediately saw the potential and proceeded, with the aid of transport consultancy company McCormick Rankin, to convert the idea into action through the creation of a compelling strategy and persistent lobbying.

Queensland's State Government and its opposition, in a rare act of bipartisan support, funded and constructed the busway and five short years after the idea was germinated, a high frequency bus service was running on an 18km transit-only right of way, servicing 11 quality stations. In the first year of service an additional 1 million passengers used Brisbane Transport buses – numbers unheard of in the past.

The Citycat service too has helped in no small way to improve not only the ease of travel around the city but also its vitality, youthful and progressive image and linkages between the built environment and the river.

Hayes took advantage of the timely combination of improved catamaran vessel design, opportunities to improve ferry services and the opening up of riverside development to build a signature service with new quality vessels and simple clock face timetables. The result has been a staggering threefold increase in patronage in just a couple of years with business people, students and tourists alike taking advantage of the service. Property values too have jumped at strategic locations along the river pontoon where access is available.

These two services are by no means the only examples of Hayes' extraordinary leadership but do represent strong symbols of her special ability to turn ideas into results, and explain why transit experts are now regular visitors to Brisbane.

Professor Jan Gehl

Professor Jan Gehl is known throughout the world for his work on public space and public life and the systematic methodology he has developed for making the people who use cities more valuable in the city planning process. He is passionate about this and works endlessly to reclaim city centres back from the invasion of the car.

In this connection, his life-long work in Copenhagen has a special place. Throughout the many years of public space/public life research, carried out in the Copenhagen School of Architecture, the city centre of Copenhagen has been the test bed for the research, surveys and implementation. This has meant that for over 30 years the city has been reclaiming its squares and streets back from the car for public space and public life. This has transformed the city centre.

Gehl has gone on to apply the experience all over the world in Stockholm, Oslo, Riga, Edinburgh and Perth, Melbourne and Adelaide in Australia.

In 1971 Gehl published his seminal work on *Life between Buildings* which has been repeatedly

used and republished and is now available in eleven languages. He is a visiting professor in universities in Europe, North and Central America, Asia, Africa and Australia. Gehl lectures all over the world to get the message across to many people. His international experiences have lately been collected and published in the book *New City Spaces* by Jan Gehl and Lars Gemze, which describes the public space strategies in nine selected cities from five continents as well as presenting 39 specially interesting public space examples.

Gehl is an inspiration to listen to; he has shown

great commitment, vision and leadership; both his teachings and studies have transformed many city centres into places for people to enjoy.

Professor David Begg

From 1994 to 1999 Professor David Begg was Convenor of the Transportation Committee, firstly for the Lothian Regional Council and then for the City of Edinburgh Council, Scotland. During this period he led a high profile campaign to transform the way

transport policy was developed and implemented.

Policies included the first example of the reallocation of road space in the UK for more people and more public transport. The pavements of the Royal Mile were widened to encourage outdoor cafés and street entertainment and Greenways were introduced, a highly successful bus priority scheme along three of the main radials of the city. He also introduced the first Community Car Club in the UK. A radical new policy document was put together, entitled *Moving Forward* which sets new policies and targets for a five-year period. He started the process of introducing road user charging to the city and formed SESTRANS (the South East of Scotland Transport Partnership) to develop regional transport policy.

Since leaving Edinburgh he has led the UK government's advisory body, the Commission for Integrated Transport (CfIT) which monitors progress and advises government on its transport practices and programmes. Under his leadership CfIT has published a range of reports, for example *Public*

Subsidy for the Bus Industry and recommended a new method of paying for road use that could reduce road congestion across the UK by up to 44%, without decreasing the overall tax income. He also advised government during the preparation of their Transport 10-year Plan.

Begg is also a professor and Director of the Centre for Transport Policy at the Robert Gordon University in Aberdeen where he oversees an active research and conference programme. He is a non-executive member of the Strategic Rail Authority Board and a board member of Transport for London.

It is not often that one person can be a politician, a business professional and an academic, but that is what Begg offers. Over the years he has shown leadership, bravery and commitment to the cause of sustainable transport against serious opposition.

Charles A Hales

Charles Hales led the team that constructed America's first new streetcar line in 50 years, in Portland, Oregon, USA. Through a unique inter agency/private partner agreement and a fast-track design and build approach, Hales and his team also constructed a 5 mile, $150 million expansion of Portland's Light Rail System to serve the international airport.

The Portland Streetcar and the light rail extension were both, in part, privately funded. The $55 million Streetcar utilised innovative financial plans, construction techniques, vehicle procurement and

operating procedures. As a member of a five-member leadership team for the light rail expansion he helped create a partnership between the city, the local port authority, the regional transit agency, the state DOT and Bechtel Enterprises. Like the Streetcar itself, the project was constructed with only minimal federal transport funds. It utilised a development agreement and a design and build relationship with Bechtel for a new business park at the airport.

Hales supports his transport initiative with leadership on the City of Portland's brownfields redevelopment initiatives and also the building of liveable communities throughout the city. As Commissioner-in-Charge for the City of Portland's Bureau of Planning and Transport, Hales has established his reputation as a champion in the integration of land use planning and transportation.

In addition to his strategic planning, transport planning and project management work, Hales leads the Streetcar Partnership, a service to communities throughout North America that are trying to bring back this cost-effective, neighbourhood-scale transit option.

Hales brings innovation, enthusiasm, commitment and experience to the fields of transportation and planning. His leading of the Streetcar and light rail projects in Portland, Oregon is an inspiration to governments, professionals and communities around the world.

Jamie Lerner

The Brazilian architect Jamie Lerner was elected President of the International Union of Architects by the Union's General Assembly. He took up his duties, for a period of three years, at the 97th session of the UIA Council on 30 July 2002.

Born in Curitiba, capital of the State of Parana, in 1937, Jaime Lerner graduated in architecture and urban planning from the School of Architecture of the Federal University of Parana in 1964.

Responsible for the creation of the Institute of

Urban Planning and Research of Curitiba (IPPCU) in 1965, he participated in the preparation of the master plan for the capital of Parana that resulted in its physical, economic and cultural transformation. He was elected mayor of the city for three terms: 1971/75, 1979/83 and 1989/92.

During his first term as Mayor of Curitiba, he consolidated the urban transformation of the city and implemented the Integrated Mass Transport System, acknowledged worldwide for its efficiency, quality and low cost. During his two ensuing terms, in addition to pursuing his innovative urban planning, Lerner intensified the social

measures that place Curitiba among the capitals of the world with the highest quality of life.

Elected Governor of Parana in 1994, re-elected in 1998, Jaime Lerner promoted the greatest economic and social transformation in the history of the state through a programme encompassing the issues of land use, transport, sanitation, health, education, recreation and culture.

Lerner teaches at the School of Architecture and Urban Planning of the Federal University of Parana and at the University of Berkeley. He is a United Nations consultant in urban planning and winner of many awards and distinctions, notably: the United Nations Environment Award, in 1990; the 1996 UNICEF Children and Peace Award; the Netherlands Prince Claus Award for Culture and Development in 2000; the World Technology Award from the National Museum of Science and Industry (London), in 2001.

Lerner is also winner of the UIA Sir Robert Matthew Prize for Improvement in the Quality of Human Settlements, which was officially presented to him on 25 July 2002(?), during the UIA Congress in Berlin.

Joan Clos Matheu

Joan Clos was first elected Mayor of Barcelona in September 1997. He was also elected President of the Metropolitan Area of Barcelona under the same mandate.

He holds a number of international posts concerned with municipal and urban policy, in addition to his role as President of the Metropolis. He is President of the Advisory Committee of Local Authorities of the United Nations, President of the World Association of Cities and Local Authorities Co-ordination (WACLAC), and Member of the Committee of the Regions of the European Union. He is Vice-president of the Executive Bureau of the Council of Municipalities and Regions of Europe (CMRE), Vice-president of the United Towns Organisation (UTO) and Member of the Executive Committee of the International Union of Local Authorities (IULA).

Joan Clos was born in Parets del Vallès (Barcelona) on 29 June 1949. He is married and has two children.

He began his work in Barcelona city government in 1979 as director of the city's Public Health Department and then was named Co-ordinator for Public Health. In 1983, he was elected to the city

council of Barcelona and was made Director of Public Health.

In 1987, he was named Councillor-president of Ciutat Vella (Old City) District Council, a position from which he would guide the conversion of the historic centre of Barcelona. Regeneration of such a derelict area was achieved by the combination of a shift to a sustainable and citizen-friendly urban planning and the promotion of a widespread network of cultural facilities. In June 1991, he was promoted to second-deputy mayor, with the responsibility for organisational structure and economy.

After the municipal elections of 1995, he was named first-deputy mayor and President of the Treasury and Infrastructure Commission. As head of the city's finances, he brought about significant reduction in municipal debt and produced budget surpluses in the annual accounts.
As Mayor, his priorities include:

- improving the city's infrastructure, by enlarging the airport and bringing a high-speed train route that links Barcelona to both Madrid and Paris;
- providing the leadership and structure for the co-ordination of public policy throughout the metropolitan region of Barcelona;
- maintaining and improving Barcelona's attractions as a tourist destination, a centre of culture and leisure activities and as a liveable city of human scale that provides a wonderful quality of life;
- attracting new high-tech industry to locate in Barcelona by providing a highly skilled workforce and receptive climate for international business activities;
- following Barcelona's success as the site of the 1992 Olympics, to provide the setting for the Universal Forum of Cultures in 2004.

His leadership and vision have transformed the old town of the city and been an inspiration to many people around the world.

ESSENTIAL BIBLIOGRAPHY

Barcelona
Barcelona Espai Públic, Ajuntament de Barcelona 1992

Boston
Benjamin Thompson & Partners, *Process: Architecture*, No 89, 1990.
Donald Lyndon, *The City Observed: Boston*, New York: Vintage Books, 1982.

Brisbane
Queensland Government, Queensland Transport. Fact Sheets

Bristol
Andrew Kelly, *Bristol Legible Cities*, Bristol Cultural Development Partnership.
Andrew Kelly & Mekanie Kelly, *Managing Partnerships. Bristol Cultural Development Partnership.*
Bristol Legible City 2001. Bristol City Council.

Copenhagen
Jan Gehl and Lars Gemzoe, *Building Public Spaces – Public Life*, Dep. of Urban Design, School of Architecture, Royal Danish Academy of Fine Arts, Denmark.
Urban Make, Strategies for Central Areas of Copenhagen, KAF, 1996.

Edinburgh
Greenways Information Pack, The City of Edinburgh Council.

Glasgow
Glasgow City Centre Public Realm. Strathclyde Regional Council, 1995.

Gothenburg
Henry Miles, 'Bus Stop', *Architectural Review*, March 1997.
Neils Torp Arkitekter MNAL, *Norsk Arkitekturmuseum*, 1997.

Hong Kong
Peter Davey, 'Travelling Light', *Architectural Review*, September 1998.

Lisbon
John E Linden, 'Orient Express', *Architectural Review*, July 1998.

New York
Grand Central Partnership Creates a New Midtown District, Institute for Urban Design, August 1991.
New Life for a Midtown Business District, Institute for Urban Design, September 1987.
Targets of Opportunity, 34th Street Partnership, 1992.

Oslo
Henry Miles, 'The Flying Norsemen', *Architectural Review*, May 1999.

Portland
Charlie Hales and Thomas B Furmaniak. *Portland Central City Streetcar Line*. Hales, C. Central City Streetcar. RailVolution Conference, Portland, Oreg., Sept. 1998.

Singapore
Keong, Dr. Chin Kian, *Road Pricing Singapores Experience*. Essay prepared for the third seminar of the Imprint Europe Thematic Network: "Implementing Reform on Transport, pricing: Constraints and solutions: learning from best practise." Brussels, October 2002.

TGV
Catherine Slessor, 'French Lessons, *Architectural Review*, April 2003.

Toronto
Catherine Slessor, 'Glorious Galleria', *Architectural Review*, March 1994.

Vancouver
Bo Helliwell, 'View from Vancouver', *Architectural Review*, December 2001.

Yokohama
Michael Webb, 'Cruise Control', *Architectural Review*, January 2003.
Jonathan Glancey, 'Foreign Affairs', *The Guardian*, 25th March 2002.
Rowan Moore, 'Building the Future', *Evening Standard*, 16th August 2002.

USEFUL WEBSITES
www.greatbuildings.com
www.faneuilhallmarketplace.com
www.pressleyinc.com
www.f-o-a.net
www.basilisk.com
www.fosterandpartners.com
www.south-bank.net.au
www.sydney.com.au
www.pps.org
www.therocks.com

PHOTOGRAPHIC CREDITS

p.6, Air Force/Genesis Space Photo Library; pp.8–9, © Mario Bettella; p.10 left, Paul A Souders/CORBIS; p.16, © Yab Arthus-Bertrand/CORBIS; p.17, © Nicole Katano; p.19, © Bill Ross/CORBIS; p.21, © Jonathan Blair/CORBIS; p.22 © Bob Krist/CORBIS; p. 24–5, © Paul Bock; p. 28 © Clear Channel Norway, p.29, pp.30–1 Aviaplan Norway; pp.32–3 SNCF AP-AREP, Didier Boy De La Tour; pp.34–5 SNCF AP-AREP, Stéphan Lucas; p.36, SNCF AP-AREP Michel Denance; pp.38–45 © Dennis Gilbert, VIEW; pp.46-8, p.120, © Translink; p.50, 52, © Hans Wretling; p.54, 56, © Bo Zaunders/CORBIS; p.55, © Jon Hicks/CORBIS; p.57, © Catherine Karnow/CORBIS; p.58, 74 right, p.72 76, 78, 80, 85 left, 86, 89, 90, 91, 94, p.96 105, 107 left, 108 left, 117, © Neil Setchfield; p.60, © Foreign Office Architects; pp.61–4, © Sue Barr, VIEW; pp.66–9, © Paul Bock; p.74 left, 75, 104, 110, 112, 114, © pictures colour library.com; p79, South Bank Corporation; p.82, 84 right, 85 right, 87, far right, © Jan Gehl and Lars Gemzøe; p.83-4 left, © Steve Raymer/CORBIS; p.88, © Abillo Lope/CORBIS; p.92, Bob Krist/CORBIS; p.93 left, © Lee Snider/CORBIS; p.93 right, © L. Clarke/CORBIS; p.97–8 Bob Burley © Design Archive; p.100, 102 © Clear Channel Independent; p.106, © Jon Hicks/CORBIS; p.107 right, © Dave G. Houser/CORBIS; p.108 right, © Cover; p.111, © Larry Lee/CORBIS; p.113, © Robert Garvey/CORBIS; p.116 © Gunter Marx/CORBIS; p.118, © Peter Aaron; p.119, James KM Cheng Architects; p.122, © Adam Woolfitt/CORBIS; pp.123–4, p.125 left, p.125 right © Kurt Stier/CORBIS; pp.126–9 © Gillespies; pp.130-2 © 1991 Steve Rosenthal; p.138, © London Aerial Photo Library/CORBIS; pp.139–40, © Lindsay Robertson; p.142-3, 144, 146, © Fitch: London; pp.148–9, 150 © Clear Channel Adshel; pp.152–4, 155 left, 156, © Collart Herve/CORBIS SYGMA; pp.158–60, 162, © Jean Heusser/CTS 2003; p.161, © Herman R. Silbiger; pp.164–8 © Susan E. Frost; pp.170–3, © Queensland Transport; p.174, © Royalty-Free/CORBIS; pp.180–2, © atsLtd.co.uk; pp. 184-5, © Oliveiro Najmias + Luis Maria Etchegorry; p. 186, Busby + Associates Architects, photo Nic Lemoux. Picture research for pp. 8-15, 26, 70-1, 134-6, 184-6 by Mariangela Palazzi-Williams.